FORGET ME NOT

DR APARNA BARUAH

Copyright © Aparna Baruah

First published in Australia in 2023
by KMD Books
Waikiki, WA 6169

All rights reserved. No part of this book may be used or reproduced by any means, graphic, electronic, or mechanical, including photocopying, recording, taping or by any information storage retrieval system without the written permission of the copyright owner except in the case of brief quotations embodied in critical articles and reviews.

Because of the dynamic nature of the Internet, any web addresses or links contained in this book may have changed since publication and may no longer be vaild. The views expressed in this work are solely those of the author and do not necessarily reflect the views of the publisher and the publisher hereby disclaims any responsibility for them.

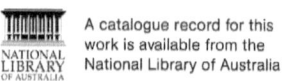

A catalogue record for this work is available from the National Library of Australia

National Library of Australia Catalogue-in-Publication data:

Forget Me Not/Dr Arparna Baruah

ISBN:
978-0-6457250-0-1
(Paperback)

This book is dedicated with deepest love to my husband, Sunny, and my boys, Adi and Arry. They inspire me to be the best version of myself.

PROLOGUE

Everyone loves to share and hear stories. I spontaneously started writing short stories in January 2020 after attending a wedding in India. Being born in India, my soul opens up with love whilst I am there, and I become a sponge soaking up new experiences. During that journey I met a stranger – a caretaker of the guesthouse where we stayed in the hills of North Bengal. His warmth touched my soul. He emulated the human emotions of love, kindness, compassion and simplicity. I penned down my interactions with him in my journal and read it aloud to my hubby and boys. To my surprise, they all felt, in their own ways, the feel-good factor – the emotion which flowed in me whilst I was writing. It was the aha moment when *Forget-Me-Not* was conceived. Soon, my mind flooded with names, moments and stories that touched my life. Each one of them tickled my soul and opened up a new perspective.

This collection of short stories is based on real people. Some of them are an integral part of my life, and some I heard about from friends and family. These simple stories emulate life in full.

They instantly stir the emotions of love, gratitude, inspiration and warmth. They are not all joyous moments; some are painful, which are transmuted by love and gratitude.

Each story will allow readers to visualise, dream, ponder and evoke an emotion. It could be the same emotion which was evoked in me, or different, but each reader will OWN the story. But the journey will be the same and so will the destination – the *feel-good factor*. These emotions are hidden within all of us, and we just need a little torch to peek at them in our busy uncertain lives. This, in turn, gives us certainty and hope and empowers us to be the best version of ourselves.

My book will be the torch to see them, touch them and feel them in your own way. The excitement, the passion, the creative outbursts which I endured whilst writing the book are magical moments which I will cherish forever. These moments allowed me to be the person I am – passionate, joyful, energetic, bursting with awe and amazement, to learn and grow. I love learning, and I learn best when I let my guards down. My novice writing journey allowed me to be a better version of myself. It was a self-exploratory journey of knowing my truth.

Don't rush the book, take your time and savour every moment!

'Life is a balance of holding on and letting go.'
– Rumi

UNSURE ALLURE

Nervously, Ana clipped her nails whilst her fingers trembled.

She was ensuring they were neatly clipped but didn't bother to file them. 'You need to have some sugar in you, so drink the milk,' shouted her roomie, Mini.

'Do I really need to? I feel nauseous,' replied Ana, still looking pretty in her polka-dotted white and green dress and crisp white lab coat.

Mini meticulously arranged a stethoscope, percussion hammer, torch and pen in a neat pile on top of Ana's bed.

A faint knock at the door made Ana skip a beat, in already racing heart. She didn't allow Mini to utter a word and rushed, barefooted, out of the room through the corridor of the girl's hostel and down a flight of stairs.

'Why did you come so late? I thought I would miss my good luck charm and my medicine exam would be a disaster.' Tears rolled out of her hazel brown eyes, with lashes so long they cluttered together, giving them more depth. Her smooth skin, which was not well hydrated due to the stress of the exams, still had a silky glow and her emotions brought a pinkish hue to her high cheekbones.

Vivek knew the face too well and could read what was going on, so without delay he held her gently at her elbows and planted a caring kiss on her forehead. He softly muttered, 'Good luck, my dear,' and left.

Ana ran inside, feeling like breaking up the fearful shackles which bound her on days of her exams. She splashed water on her cheeks. Still wet and sticky, she was ordered by Mini to neatly tie up her hair and pick up her belongings. Mini held the glass of milk close to Ana's face and she had a few gulps of it, feeling the milk curdling instantly with the enormous build up of acid in her digestive tract.

***

Later in the day, Vivek ordered a plate of Haka noodles and chilli chicken; a meal that hadn't changed over five years of their post-exam catch up. It was a cold winter evening and Ana looked cosy in her pink high-necked jumper. They both savoured the food whilst laughing out loud, listening to the silly answers Ana had voiced in her oral examination. She also checked out the correct diagnosis and the management plan for the long and short cases she was examined on, but Vivek just kept staring at her. He allowed her to blabber relentlessly tonight, since he knew she needed the verbal diarrhoea as a relaxation.

Often they spoke and argued for hours on topics as varied as music, movies, medicine, fashion, dreams, fantasies, family and friends, but there was an unstated rule; Ana had to have the last say.

Vivek had always sparked chemistry with the opposite sex, whether young or old. His perfect square jawline was his most attractive feature, along with his ruffled hair and sharp nose. He had a rather sharp mind and the gift of the gab, which drew everyone's attention. A certain unnamed trait of his personality drew people to engage, interact and connect with him.

They hadn't seen each other for nearly a month since Vivek was a new intern busy with night shifts, while Ana had clinics, exams and a boyfriend who needed much attention.

Vivek held Ana`s hands firmly and led her to his motorbike, speeding her away to the nearest ice cream parlour. He ordered her favourite flavour of rum and raisin and specified, before Ana could speak, 'one scoop only'. They smiled at each other whilst Vivek again had to listen to relentless stories of how enchanting her dream man, Sanjay, was. Vivek was currently dating Simi and Ana was reluctant to acknowledge that she was the best fit for him.

Ana and Vivek were strangers and happened to connect accidentally in the University. Vivek was her senior and guided her in tutorials and academics. Their interactions were rare at the outset, but when they met, they immediately felt they were the best of buddies. They both had partners whom they dated, but shared their crushes, romantic visions and break-ups with each other. They each relied on the other emotionally; their relationship was more friendship, with a hint of romanticism. There was an unknown chemistry between them which gently evolved as spontaneous, fun and unnamed.

***

Sanjay waved goodbye to Ana as he walked out the front door. 'It's date night today, so I should be back on time.' Their six-year-old daughter yelled, 'Mum, are you ready? We'll be late for school.' Ana jumped up from the wrought iron chair in her back garden and looked at her watch. Quickly picking up the Merc keys, she adjusted her yoga pants and rushed to the car. The five minute drive to school felt like an hour, since she was in complete silence. Her mind was racing, trying to find the exact name for her relationship with Vivek, as she was penning down her memories in her diary for her short story collection. A relationship so complex yet simple. Vivid yet vague. Secure yet fragile. Tender yet callous. Was this a chemistry to be remembered, or a chemical reaction which vanished?

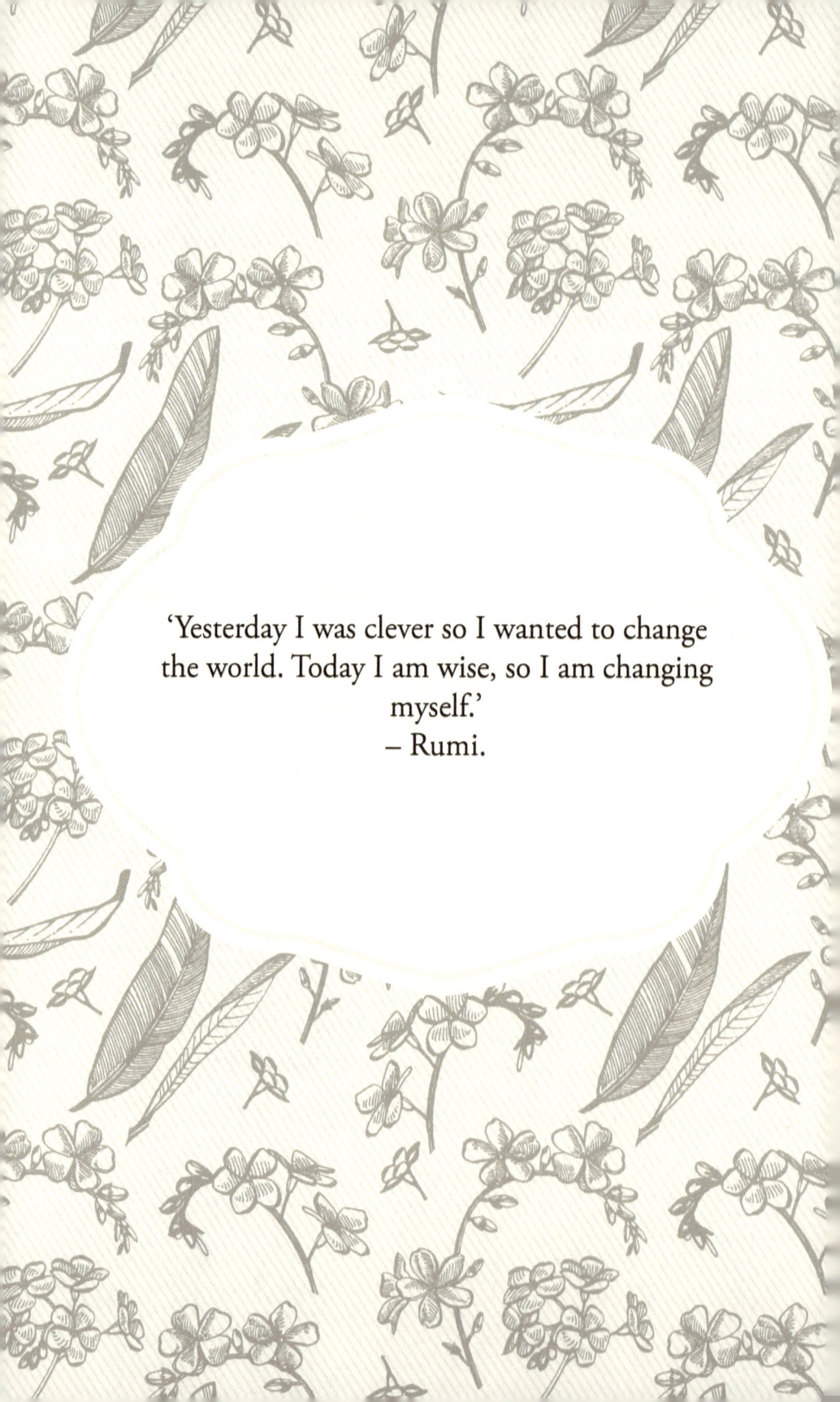

'Yesterday I was clever so I wanted to change the world. Today I am wise, so I am changing myself.'
– Rumi.

A SLICE OF CAKE

The rising golden yellow hue, with a few fine cracks, brought on an exciting feeling. The ground glass and a few steel racks did block the view a little, but in its entirety, it appeared perfect. Maya adorned a green pair of silicon gloves and was looking at it with a certain knowingness. This is the perfect time for it to come out, but she trusted her gut and said to herself, 'a few more minutes …' On the black marble tabletop was a bottle of brown elixir and Maya put on her glasses to confirm it was, indeed, 'organic' and from Mrs. Maple's store.

The lingering aroma heightened her senses and brought up a mixed bag of emotions; she didn't know which one predominated. She turned off the oven and glanced at the golden beauty once again and smiled.

She sat on her favourite red Victorian chair, that overlooked her manicured garden, full of blooms in early spring. Even the weeds had flowers, she noticed. She picked up her diary to pen a few words. It was already five minutes and remembering Delia Smith's strict instructions on 'how to bake a perfect Victorian Sponge cake', she lovingly took the cake out and settled it over a cooling rack. Maya was meticulous in this role since she took great pride in releasing both layers of the cake perfectly. It indeed untethered her soul.

Maya sat down with her diary and looked out. Her mind was blank, yet full of memories which flashed in front of her eyes. She gazed at the garden waiting for a creative outburst to pen her next story, but the aroma of the freshly baked vanilla-essenced beauty engulfed her senses and she stared at the perfectly baked cake in delight. She knew she had to have a decadent slice first, with a cup of tea, to get her creative juices flowing.

She layered the cake with fresh strawberry jam, reorganised them perfectly to stack, and dusted some icing sugar on top. It looked like a 'Delia' cake sitting daintily on the white cake stand. Maya licked her fingers in delight and grabbed her phone to take a picture of her creation for her next Instagram post.

She fondly cut the cake and put the kettle on to make herself a perfect cup of English breakfast tea. She sliced the cake neatly into eight pieces and was wondering which slice to pick when all of a sudden, a story surfaced in her soul. She pondered for a moment and then thought of the fascinating fable her grandfather had told her as a child. She picked up her pen and settled into writing the story.

***

There was once a man who'd had a very long and tiring day at work. He was exhausted and hungry and rushed to his local bakery just before the owner was ready to close. There was nothing much left apart from a medium-sized cake. He rushed home and cut the cake into eight slices and wondered which slice he should eat first. He labelled the slices in his mind and set about eating them in this order. He ate the fourth slice first, then the seventh slice, then the fifth, the second, the third, the sixth and the first. He was still not satisfied and finally picked up the eighth slice. As soon as he ate the eighth slice, he was totally satisfied. An outburst of joy, peace and relaxation filled his soul. However, he had an insight and thought, 'How foolish am I? I should have eaten the eighth slice first, and then I would have been instantly satisfied. I wasted all the other slices which I could have savoured throughout the week!' The very thought made him miserable and he lost his Satori moment.

***

Grandad had narrated the story to Maya when she was a confused teenager. 'Dear Maya,' he said, 'life is like this. You have to have diverse experiences in life which make you complete. Your past experiences are the slices of the cake, each of which are equally important in making the person you are. You can't choose a slice of life that was better than the others and ignore the rest. Life too is beautiful, where every slice of your life, be it victories or challenges, will equally contribute to making the amazing being you are.'

Maya loved the story and whenever she chose a slice of cake she fondly remembered Grandad's story and its message.

We all are beautiful in our own way. The holes make us

whole and the cracks strengthen us. The total package of who we are includes all our experiences, which have enriched us to bring out our unique flavour. Be authentically YOU!

'The wound is the place where
the light enters you.'
– Rumi

E-LATIONSHIP

Remo yawned and looked at the time. It was 2am and yet he had six more hours of support to offer. Bored with the monotony of his work, life and the sounds of eternal night, he lit another cigarette. He was aware that he was smoking way too much but didn't want to admit it. In fact, smoking gave him short bursts of release from his captured self and a sense of imminent freedom.

He sluggishly looked at his laptop. The IT helpdesk work log was trivial. He affirmed that the night would be long and cold. The US was in the midst of peak winter and it was not as busy as pre-Christmas days.

He hated such silences and gaps in his work, since his mind would drift back to his past. He took a deep sigh and laid in the crisp and cold bed. He drew a blanket over him. His favourite pastime was gazing at the ceiling, which he did often, a kind of mindfulness meditation. But what he did was pray and visualise that his life would be touched by the miracle of pure love.

Remo jumped up and realised that more than an hour had passed, as he heard the faint chirping of the birds before dawn. He quickly logged in and breathed a sigh of relief. Work was negligible and he was now ready to take a break. He opened up the already logged-in Instagram page and he unconsciously checked the posts and sent new requests for friendship.

Remo wondered to himself, 'Is this the life of a divorcee?" He was fed up trying to rebuild a new life in his home country, returning from living overseas for ten years. Everything was old yet new. It was a strange feeling, and nothing brought him peace. Everything felt empty and worthless, but his relationship with God was unfathomable. His faith in the superpower kept his heart open, although his mind was closed: definitely no marriage and no relationship.

'Can we be friends? I come from a respectable family and I am an IT engineer.' The message was sent a month ago. Instagram messenger general list read: waiting for request to be accepted.

***

'The camera angle is not right. Please can you not capture me so close?' Anna was always busy and the perfection gene bugged her. 'Do you think a podcast host is an easy job?' she laughed out loud to her bestie who reminded her of their lunch catch up. Rushing down the stairs to make it in time, she glanced into the mirror and smiled. The smile was her accessory and no matter what, she could lift the corners of mouth with ease. Not really satisfied with her look, but very content in her new role as a script creator, she felt appreciative of the opportunity.

A glimpse of pride made her smile but she was totally aware this was not her primary role. She guided the Uber driver and glanced at her phone to check her notifications.

'OMG social media – am I enjoying this?' she said to herself, as she looked at her friend requests. She switched it off and instantly went back to the request page, adding a few names in the list. Back home after a long day and putting the kids to bed she laid down in Joe's lap, narrating the whole day in such detail that Joe thought it was rather musical.

Anna was new to social media platforms and was learning to interact with her new-found fan following. The majority of them she sent an emoji of thanks, but time and again her eyes were drawn to a message which read, 'Can we be friends? I come from a respectable family and I am an IT engineer.' She looked at the profile picture – decent and honest was her impression. She accepted Remo's request and replied back, 'Are you an Italian too?'

Every relation is unique, and this was no different. Their friendship was spontaneous, honest and liberating. They shared the stories that owned them, and revealed every truth like children do. There was no pretence in the chats over messenger and phone calls. Remo addressed Anna as a 'gift from the Almighty' and convinced her he could feel her energy, wherever she was. A few surreal episodes happened in which Remo came into Anna's dreams, to the vivid extent that they both began to believe in a past soul connection. Romance blossomed in Remo's mind and he possessed her with his passion. The estranged Anna resisted and found new ways of confronting Remo. She was scared to feel this new emotion which she couldn't label. Being a control freak, she struggled to entertain the new acquaintance who opened her vulnerability. She lost her will to be perfect and enjoyed evolving in her life.

Remo taught her to open her wounds, which are, indeed, 'windows of healing', as Rumi quotes. Nothing changed for Anna in her real world apart from Remo being a mirror for her soul. She became a more committed wife and mother, her caring nature towards life surfaced like a new dawn.

The assignment given to them by the universe unfolded them in two separate directions. Anna became unbounded and free from her set ways and Remo committed to have a healthy life, acknowledging her as his soul lover.

***

It was the summer of 2022 – two years post-Covid. Anna booked her tickets for Florence. Travelling from Australia is never easy, no matter where you go, but especially to Europe. Remo's phone was often engaged and lately he had become busy at work too. Anna didn't think or plan much since they had decided on a unique meeting with no expectations – only love.

Sitting comfortably in the plane, she was secure knowing that in spite of being a married woman, the person she was reaching out to was somebody she loved. But although she said this to herself, she was aware that she had to keep her romantic inclinations in check, to fulfil the vows of a loyal marriage where she was adored and respected.

A flashback of memories stirred mixed emotions within her. She fondly recollected moments of laughter, fights, complaints, emotional outbursts, romantic inclinations, all the normal stuff that happens in a relationship. But she also realised what Remo had taught her over the last two years in a virtual relationship.

She learnt from him what pure love and its energy was about. Remo's love for her had no expectations, no bondage, no feeling of separation; the love that resides in the core of every one of us.

The plane landed smoothly and Anna looked out of the window in anticipation and excitement. *What would Remo be like in reality?* She checked out her luggage and looked at Peretola Airport with a numbness that engulfed her. Her energy was suddenly sad.

She denied the feeling, saying to herself, 'It's the long journey' and confidently walked out. Remo did say he would wait at the entrance. She pondered a few moments, looked carefully at names and signs while the Italian language muffled her ears. She picked up the phone and rang him …

An elderly man had a bunch of flowers in his hand and asked, 'Anna? Are you looking for someone?'

Anna vehemently said, 'Yes.' To which he replied, 'I have a message for you,' and handed over an envelope. Anna's hand was shaking as she opened the envelope, and an intense sadness filled her. Tears rolled from her eyes, she knew.

The message read: 'Lovers don't finally meet somewhere. They are in each other all along. Go back home safely Anna. Love you.'

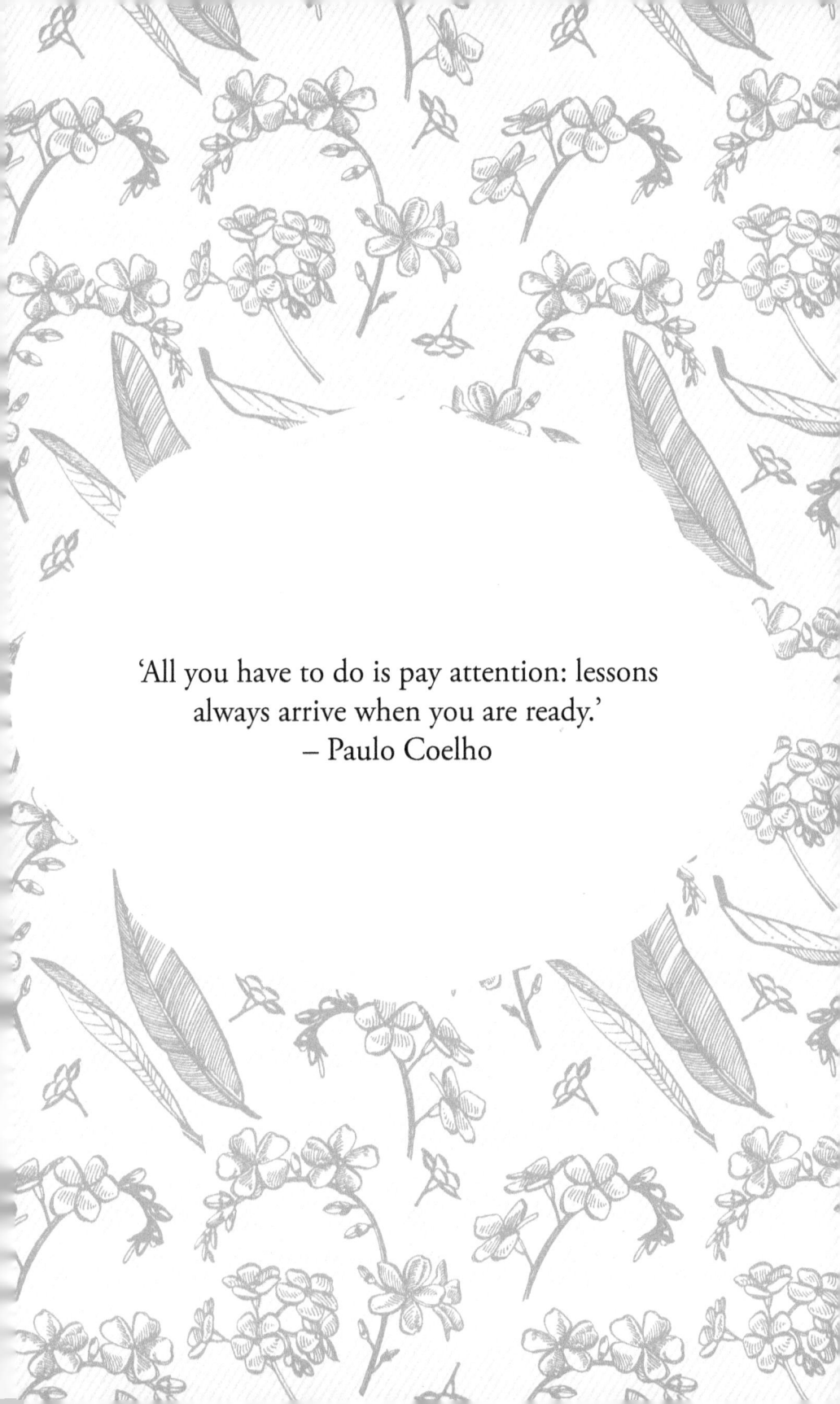

'All you have to do is pay attention: lessons always arrive when you are ready.'
– Paulo Coelho

EMBRACE

How often have you seen birds?
How often have you noticed them?
How often have you observed them?
How often have you admired them?
How often have you listened to them?
Please pause before you read ahead and own your answers.

I hadn't seen them until recently. I wondered why it took four decades for me to see them! I really don't have an answer and that is exactly what I'm exploring. I am teaching myself to see birds once again.

I did notice them in my childhood, but somehow they disappeared in my youth. I do remember seeing a few of them while visiting zoos and bird sanctuaries when travelling the world; the exotic ones, especially in Singapore where I pictured myself. However, I am still trying to find the answer to my previous questions.

I wrote this piece when I took the opportunity to slow down amidst my work. I realised that lately I've been making efforts to reconnect with myself. I was surprised that I didn't need to get out to admire the world outside to open my heart. I could instead rely on my deepest experiences, which continue to instil such vivid impressions in my mind.

Now, I see birds of different hues, hopping with their delicate feet and flying on invisible strings. I admire how unique their features are and how each one has a different expression. I have keenly observed how they interact with me; some with love, apprehension or wonder. I have often felt that some do understand my feelings. I am convinced they can hear, since they sing along during my music sessions. I often attentively listen to them and each one sings straight to the soul. This guides me to find my voice and share my truth with the world.

Have you noticed the flight of the birds? They soar and glide with the certainty that the wind will gently guide them around the branches. They flap their wings with such confidence and effortless ease. They trust their landings even if they are close to a cage. Their uncertainty makes them certain. Their effortlessness generates trust. As I watch them flying with awe and love, I realise that their beating wings calm my beating heart.

This is the moment, yes, the very moment when I EMBRACE life. And so do you, in all its beauty, magic and mysticism. Every day we are offered countless opportunities to deeply experience the world around us. We have to be ready to slow down and embrace the freedom these magical beauties offer. Do it today!

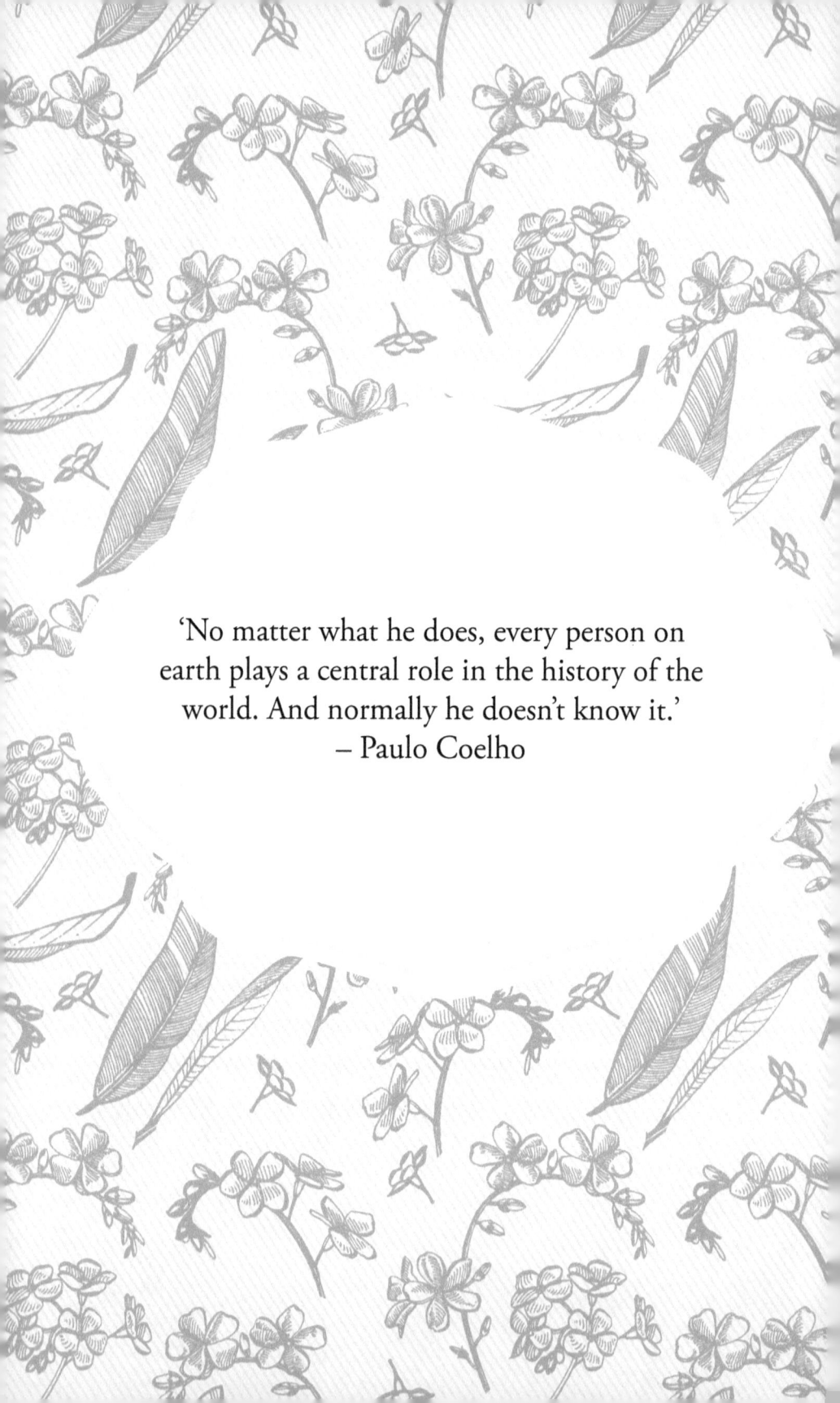

'No matter what he does, every person on earth plays a central role in the history of the world. And normally he doesn't know it.'
– Paulo Coelho

FAITH ON THEFT

The excitement was palpable amongst the adults. The kids were tired and exhausted, and parents took turns to moniter them in the queue. There were some 50,000 people in the queue, within our sight. It was already eight hours of gradual progression and we were nearly there. The last leg of the journey, as we all know, is the most impatient. The experience was unique, consuming all our senses.

We could now faintly hear the prayers being recited and hear the bells. We were in a state of spiritual ecstasy that we would soon get a glimpse of the Divine Sri Venkateswara at the Tirupati Balaji temple. And finally pushing through the crowd while being in a trance of divinity, we did get a glimpse of the omnipotent, omnipresent power. I looked at our creator in all His glory and the exchange of energy was magnificent. All our tiredness, irritation, frustration, hunger, thirst and soreness in our bare feet, waiting in the crowded queue of 50,000 people, disappeared in a glimpse. Experiences like these unify us, and allow us to savour the eternal truth that we are all one.

This moment of surrender is what we all seek when visiting places of worship or faith.

This temple is gloriously described by the Hindu scriptures as the earthly location where Lord Vishnu resides. It's one of the most pivotal landmarks of the Hindu mythology. Notably, it's the most popular temple on the Earth today, with a maximum number of devotees visiting on any given day. It's also the richest temple in the world, attracting the largest amount of donations on a daily basis. It is believed that all your wishes are fulfilled here. It is customary practice to offer your hair as a donation, along with your promised contributions, once wishes are fulfilled.

In ancient India, temples were built as energy centres which reverberated with a powerful source of energy. Temples were built, based on a certain science called Agama. The five basic parameters included size and shape of the temple, the sanctum, the idol, the Mudra that the idol holds and the mantras that are used to consecrate. If these things are properly matched, it creates a tremendous field of energy. The essence was that people would spend some time in the morning and evening within this strong field of energy and imbibe it. This energy is like a battery charger which allows us to recharge and recalibrate whilst riding through life.

We felt blessed, getting an opportunity to visit the temple and learn all about its 3,000 years of history. We were tired and exhausted having woken at 4am, yet after the Darshan (beholding the Lord), we were all rejuvenated. We planned to visit the donation site and humbly offer our contribution. The place was overcrowded with devotees, some carrying bags of money and others jewellery to offer as donations. My hubby and I were ready to make our donations, when suddenly he realised his wallet was empty.

To our surprise and dismay, we rushed to check each other's purses and pockets, however we clearly remembered we had kept the entire intended donation of 20,000 Indian rupees, separately in an envelope. This was a very precious, once-in-a-lifetime visit to the holy shrine and we were rather organised. We realised we had been pickpocketed. The reality was a predicament. We were initially upset and saddened, but we did have a shift in our response. We both decided we were of service to someone who needed the money desperately. This was surrender in the presence of the Divine. We didn't judge the person or the situation but believed in the bigger purpose. We forgave the person who braved such an act in such a divine boundary. We borrowed our donations from our brother-in-law and offered our contribution.

Every experience can open our connection with the universe. Teachers are all around us and if you have an open mind to learn and grow, even an obstacle will be an opportunity for growth. The visit to the temple remained extra-special, since we felt we had, made a contribution to someone who needed it.

'Everything in life can change except one thing: your passion.'
– Paulo Coelho

GLOBAL DESIS

'Girls your hands are uncoordinated and look at your lines,' Riya screamed. 'I am sure to lose my singing voice.'

The girls in the front row stiffened while the ladies at the rear looked amused and irritated with an infallible expression. 'Now what?'

Riya stopped the music and looked at them all with a feeling of nervousness which she pretended she didn't have. She declared with a calming authority, 'The auditions are tomorrow and we have been practising for the last three months, so what's wrong now? Do you guys really want to perform this year?'

An instant affirmation by the group came with conviction. 'Let's correct our *minor* shortcomings and concentrate.' The performers all appeared focused to perform their best, whilst having a quick chat amongst themselves.

So let's introduce you to amateur dance troupe – Global Desis (GD).

Age range: seven to forty – predominantly a female team with a couple of boys

Team formed: 2012 – sitting in a lounge having tea

Performances: 2012-2020

Team founder: hopeless enthusiast – Riya

Team members: two distinct groups

i. Enthusiastic young dancers – all trained in Indian classical, hip hop, contemporary styles

ii. Enthusiastic mums with commitment and conviction

Motivation: evening rehearsals in week days for an hour. Freedom for youngsters from schoolwork and chats over tea and snacks for mums

Team ethos: Unique and United.

***

Riya sat on her lounge, her right leg, still in pain, resting on the footstool. She smiled to herself while reading her journal about her dance group, before looking up at the horizon. Her walking stick was nearby, but it was a chore to pick it up while balancing herself. She wanted to sit outside in the cold winter's day, reminiscing on her memories of the Global Desis. As she walked past her library, her eyes laid on the beautiful cards and thank you notes written to her by the team members. Her eyes welled up with gratitude and she felt a deep sense of satisfaction.

Life does give you whatever you want when you least expect it, she thought. The enormous joy, love and respect the team had given her over ten years of her life, possessed her with such enthusiasm that she instantly began planning a get together

– reunion of the GD.

She took out her smart phone, which was smarter than anything she knew, and commanded SIRI to send a message to all the GD members for a reunion at the Fresh Water Bay School undercover area, 'this coming Saturday at 2pm'. She never thought about who would or wouldn't make it. She only knew she had a deep urge to reconnect with the group. This was the faith or conviction, which Riya carried throughout her life. Her enthusiasm for life was a magnet for all and things happened spontaneously for her.

It was a Wednesday afternoon when the message was sent, promptly hearing back from her best friend and stalwart that she would definitely be there. Riya planned in her mind to cater some beautiful cakes and savouries with some piping hot tea and dialled a few numbers to arrange it.

By the time Friday evening arrived, Riya was rather disappointed. She had received very few confirmations. A few apologies came from busy young ladies and a few health issues from her contemporaries. 'Never mind' was her current mantra.

Riya went on to recollect the memories of their dancing days and took her journal out to rewrite the story. What was so unique about the GD? What brought out the creativity, commitment , fun and enthusiasm? What united the group in spite of language, culture or age gaps? She still felt the same waves of enthusiasm and vigour to do something, to reunite the group and perform. She did feel strange reviewing her own emotions.

Riya couldn't write a word and felt restless. She stood

up and looked into the mirror. Her hair was still straight, now with a mix of greys. Her wrinkles were her expression lines and she owned them. She saw the paucity of collagen in her loose skin and marvelled at how those wrinkles were so appropriate to suit her current look. She was still proud of her everlasting smile. She took off her glasses and looked into her hazel-coloured eyes. Staring into them, the expressive power of her eyes was still the same. She felt the eyes looking back at her were timeless and ageless. She didn't feel at all different to when she was dancing in the GD team thirty-five years ago. Her eyes had the same twinkle and glitter. She smiled in glee and knew that the eyes are the mirror of the soul. The soul is eternal and it is only the body which is subject to disintegrate.

Riya picked up her journal once again and started writing about what brought the GD together. She had all the answers, finding them in the depths of her eyes.

On Saturday afternoon Riya dressed casually for the reunion. Her heart full of enthusiasm and love, she was excited to not only connect with her old teammates but had an exciting proposal in mind. To her amazement, she found the whole team gathered, chatting, laughing and complimenting each other.

Riya walked into the centre of the group as they surrounded her. She declared, 'The first rehearsal is in Usha's garage at 6pm next Wednesday. Girls, please get your childcare sorted and ladies don't forget your kneecap and wrist supports. The title of the performance will be decided later. But first, let's have a GD catch up while we enjoy the cakes and savouries.'

The noise and the buzz was recognisable, nothing had changed over the last two decades. The ladies were all talking over each other, providing solutions, although no one actually listened. The youngsters giggled and complained about work, partners and childcare. The enthusiasm, fun and joy once again uniting this unique team. They could all be free in the canvas of creativity!

'Remember that wherever your heart is, there you will find your treasure.'
– Paulo Coelho

IN THE MIDST OF TEARS

The paintings were lined up on an off-white canvas on the floor of the studio. The enthusiastic novice artists nervously looked at their work which was displayed in a gallery, perhaps for the first time. Sometimes experiences like these merge us into one, beyond race, colour, religion and age.

The students, on insistence, had to come up with different ideas on how to positively critique an artwork. It was rather difficult to use the correct art jargon for a surgeon like Chris, who was better with his scalpel than with the brush.

He gathered his courage while looking at Maya's penetrating eyes, since it was a long eight hours he'd spent with her learning the skill. He described the painting with a few quaint words, which further broadened Maya's ever-smiling grin. Nothing could take that away and nothing did, as Chris wondered how her journey was so inspirational yet surreal.

A quote by his favourite author, Paulo Coelho, dawned on him; 'And one has to understand that braveness is not the absence of fear but rather the strength to keep on going forward, despite the fear.'

He nudged Amanda gently and thanked her for gifting him with the intensive painting class, to which he would never have imagined enrolling himself in his wildest dreams. He felt restless and tired, feeling how strangers can take a toll, especially those who are sharing your journey in a most disconnected world.

The studio was perched on a hill surrounded by Eucalypt and Gum trees. The tall but slender giants were liberally covered with a silvery smooth texture, amidst minor patches of rough, tanned stains which oozed. The slim branches swayed in ecstasy to the rhythm of the gentle wind, whilst the sun kissed the myriad of leaves resembling perfect motifs in various shades of green and burnt amber. Although they were leaves of early autumn ready for the fall, they did radiate a certain sense of calmness, interweaved with strength. The owner and the paintings had some symbolism with the forest and Chris thought dynamism merged with uncertainty.

Escaping the dynamism of a surgical world and a lazy Sunday, initially made Chris jittery, but Maya's enthusiasm, optimism and brimming smile allowed him to just be himself. As the day progressed, Maya's inspirational style of teaching a subject as abstract as art brought out Chris' artfulness.

Amanda peeped occasionally at Chris' work knowing how temperamental he was, but to her surprise, his flair, style and creativity was traversing the cracks and crevices of the textured wooden board with such proficiency, that the rest of the class couldn't take their eyes off his work. She smiled to herself, pleased with her decision to bring him here on a pleasant autumn day.

Maya's stories were so potent that each word she spoke evoked emotions, which were then captured into the artwork as creativity. Chris was hesitant to bring out his emotions into his work, but the harder he tried, his paintings portrayed the forest in the most abstract form. He felt as if a part of his emotions were being painted onto the canvas after decades of holding them in. He couldn't explain the feeling, but he was dealing with an uncertain process to bring the best out of the piece. He recognised that his artwork was coming to life with his stokes and smudges, along with his supressed emotions.

The Mist Of Tears was, indeed, a piece of Maya's which was auctioned and sold in her very first exhibition. It was the work which had made her famous. Her painting spoke about pain, but it was smothered with textures of strength, hope and peace. It was born from an uncertain womb, which is the highest form of creativity.

The applaud deafened Chris' ears and Amanda literally shook her husband since his *Mist of Tears* had won the People's Choice award at the Hadley's Art Prize competition. Chris was blank as he walked to the podium holding Amanda's hand but remembering his first teachers, the forest and Maya, who had allowed him to be vulnerable.

'When you do things from your soul, you feel a river moving in you, a joy.'
– Rumi

THE CARETAKER

The fog covered the verandah of the newly built guest-house on a cold December morning. Something about it was familiar, yet it was a new experience. Shalini breathed in deeply to awaken her senses and feel the fresh morning. Her eyes were trying hard to see through the fog, but it was in vain. She wrapped her nightgown tightly around her slim waist and prodded her way down the flight of stairs. She walked up and down the corridor of the ground floor, but he was nowhere to be seen. Shalini thought to herself, 'I did remind him yesterday that I needed it at 7am.'

She pondered gently to a partly open door labelled, 'staff only'. Gently she nudged at the wooden door; there was no-one to be seen.

She couldn't believe she was in the land of the magical leaves, within miles of the best bushes in the Dooars Estates, yet she was yearning for her golden-brown concoction, brewed gently over two minutes, with a dash of white, which made the perfect cup of Darjeeling tea. Yes! She was in Jalpaiguri, close to one of the best tea estates in India, Makaibari, attending a family wedding.

Disappointed, she walked upstairs and entered her bedroom, with the door slightly ajar and whispered gently into Anand's ears, 'I just couldn't find anyone...'

To which Anand gently muttered, 'Try calling his number.'

Shalini swiftly opened her mobile, scrambled for her smudgy reading glasses and tried to dial the number. Suddenly, there was a gentle knock and Shalini swiftly went to open the door. To her amusement, there was a gentle looking middle-aged man, wearing a grey shirt and brown trousers, crowned with a grey-patterned monkey cap and muffler, smiling at her. He carried a plastic tray, flowered in white and pink, and on it were two floral ceramic cups and saucers filled with tea. On the saucers were two Good Day cookies (very popular in India); a sugary, buttery, stripped cookie, flavoured with almonds.

Shalini promptly thanked him and requested he place the cups in the lounge in front of the bedroom. She had questions; *When and where did you make it? Where were you?* But since she was parched without her first drink of the day, she quickly settled in the sofa next to Anand and sipped the golden concoction. They were both connoisseurs of tea but had significantly different ways of savouring their favourite drink. However, both agreed that the body and flavour was optimally balanced, and they indeed thought that it was one of the best cups they'd had in a very long time. Shalini finished her first cup hurriedly and ran downstairs to thank him ... and also to request a second cup.

Jaganath Babu was quietly sitting in the kitchen washing

the electric kettle. The kitchen was completely empty, no signs of cups, saucers, tea, biscuits or cutlery. In fact, the wash basin also looked fairly rugged and unused. Shalini fumbled to start a conversation with him since she was intrigued that there was not much action in the kitchen to suggest that he, himself, had made the tea. Slightly suspicious, she requested for another two cups and openly praised the quality of the tea. She looked around, once again scanning for some clue, and rushed back to her room, vividly describing the strange kitchen.

Within five minutes, the next cups of tea came up and again had the same colour and flavour. Anand savoured the cookies once more, looking at the online version of the Times of India on his new iPhone, whilst Shalini comfortably seated herself to enjoy the cuppa, while counting the calories of the cookies she dipped into the tea.

For the next four mornings, Shalini and Anand woke up to Jaganath Babu's gentle knock at precisely 7am. He wore the same attire and had the same pleasing smile. Each day, his cups of tea were as flavoursome as the day before. During casual chitchat, Shalini came to know there was no one else in the guesthouse.

The day of the wedding arrived and tired everyone, including the energetic children. Everyone had a rather late night. Shalini was so tired and although the thought was there, to remind Jaganath Babu not to wake them up with tea the following morning, in the midst of opening her saree, cumbersomely tied, and removing her make-up and jewellery, she completely forgot and slumped to bed.

Of course, the 7am knock woke Shalini up and she

grudgingly went to open the door. The cups of tea were ready, and her eyes sparkled as she looked upon the hard, brown, rustic, oval biscuits that could only be found in the roadside tea stalls of Eastern India. She couldn't stop smiling as she informed him, with child-like glee, that she loved those biscuits and hadn't had them since her childhood. She promptly requested to have some more with her second cup of tea.

Shalini was excited with the little things in life and everything was a 'felt' experience for her. She enthusiastically woke up Anand and told him what an interesting surprise awaited him. Anand, a gentleman to the core, never really understood Shalini's enthusiasms of life and was often intrigued by her childlike behaviour. But being her partner for over twenty years, he got used to some of her ways, as we all do. Shalini dipped the biscuits in her tea and snatched an extra one from Anand, savouring the taste, with her eyes closed. The flavour and texture was familiar and she was in a state of deja vu.

It was over half an hour and the next cuppa had not arrived. Shalini stood up lazily amidst her descriptive mood of how and when she'd had those special biscuits, whose name she tried to remember. She came up with umpteen names, though none touched the chord.

Anand wandered around to find out what was taking so long to get his second cup of hot tea. He came back in a rather surprised mood and informed Shalini that Jaganath Babu had biked to the roadside stall some 5km away to get the biscuits for her. The kitchen aid had said that since the cookie box was empty the night before, he had got some of the roadside biscuits while riding to work. He never thought that 'Mam' would appreciate them so much, so he rushed out to bring her some more kata biscuits from the same stall, which was approximately half an hour ride away.

The gesture touched Anand and Shalini. In a few minutes, she could hear footsteps, and in a pensive mood Shalini went out to receive her second cuppa from Jaganath Babu's hand. This time her heart was full of appreciation and gratitude, emotions that make our living so worthwhile.

The car was packed with the help of Jaganath Babu and his aids, helping to load the rooftop carrier with luggage for Bagdogra airport. Jaganath Babu asked Shalini how life was in Australia. She learnt that he had postponed his wife's medical trip to Bangalore to attend to the guests for a week. On understanding the details from a medic's prospective, Shalini came to learn that his wife had serious cardiac issues requiring major surgery. He also had young children and elderly parents to care for.

Shalini was overwhelmed by the warmth which Jaganath Babu showered in spite of personal challenges. He went beyond the call of duty and made strangers feel at home with his subtle presence.

She once again affirmed her belief that going beyond what was expected was how a person decided if life was meaningful enough. She lovingly remembered the kata biscuits and her childhood memories through the meandering roads lined with Sal Forest, en route to Bagdogra.

Our paths might never meet again but Jaganath Babu would always remain my inspiration to be an author.

'Love is the bridge between you and everything.'
– Rumi

A LETTER TO MY OWN

My thoughts on seeing my seventeen-year-old son getting ready for his Year 12 ball …

You have grown into a responsible, handsome young man. I did want your haircut to be a smidge shorter, so your beautiful expressive eyes could be seen better, but trends have to be followed, I guess. Yet you look perfect, and your dimples will definitely be the highlight tonight.

I am so confident in you, Son, that I don't want to give you any instructions or sermons on how to manage yourself. I am sitting calmly over my cup of tea seeing your dad finally adjusting your shirt's collar. You both look like brothers now and interact as friends. The pleasure is immense.

But I wish I'd had a little bit more of your time during the last year. The drives to and from school are short and lately, the tuition runs have been silent meditation. I often admire you for your discipline, your focus, commitment to your work and extra-curricular activities. But deep down, I want you to be snug beside us on a couch and express your day with ease.

No frills or facts, just mundane conversation. No goal setting, just chatting about your likes and dislikes.

It was a proud moment when you told us a few years ago to 'please allow me to make my own mistakes. You guys are overprotective. I need to learn from my mistakes.' It was a rather startling statement and your dad and I had mixed feelings. We pretended we loved your mature thoughts, but deep down felt apprehensive, knowing you're growing up, facing reality, dealing with people, overcoming failures and being humbled with successes. It is a mixed emotional bag and today when I look at you, I am so proud to see that you are steering your way through life, confidently, in your own way.

Did I tell you how proud we are of your attitude towards life-focused and self reliant? Less of a moaner and that's what we admire; your resilience.

But as soon as I get a glimpse of your untidy room, I do get frustrated, silently wondering when I will walk into your room and be surprised! Lately I am perturbed you are having coffee on an empty stomach.

I wish we could have longer conversations, especially your jokes, pulling the leg of your younger brother, some of the best laughs we've had around the dinner table. Don't ever lose your humour; it's your best accessory.

I can see that you're now ready to go off to your ball. The excitement in your eyes is obvious. You are one of the most handsome boys I have seen in my lifetime (every mum says that) and you don't need to be shy about that!

From a distance, I can see you have become busy with your date and mates.

I know you are carrying all our love, values and faith with you wherever you go, and that's what makes me so proud to be your mum.

Could our monosyllabic conversations get a bit longer after Year 12?

I'm hoping we can plan a few holidays together and just sit in the backyard chatting about life whilst you are kicking a ball.

I just wanted to say, 'I love you, Son.' Be the person you are born to be.

'Remember that wherever your heart is, there you will find your treasure.'
– Pualo Coelho.

THE BIRIYANI HOME

It was a lazy Sunday morning in a twin-Victorian townhouse in Birmingham. Everyone called him Uncle – aka – Dr Daya Bora. He was a popular GP who migrated to the UK in the 70s. Doctors were then served tea in silver pots in the hospital cafés, as narrated by Uncle. However, times were different now in the NHS, in the late 90s. We were being ruled by the management of the National Health Service, a totally different scene.

Daya in 'Sanskrit' language means *kindness* and he was the embodiment of it.

A largish body frame with a gentle face, always beaming with a smile, his loving, kind, caring, thoughtful, non-judgemental nature vividly described his personality. No one could miss his open-hearted laughter and his rather loud voice, which all of us were addicted to. His patients all wanted to see Dr Bora, who emanated warmth and empathy. They loved him and made friends with him instantly.

Let's get back to the Sunday morning scene. The

twelve-seater dining table fills slowly with nieces, nephews and their friends, some of them just being introduced to the couple. Uncle and Aunty were completely unaware that these friends slept over last night! English breakfast was being made especially by Uncle, with Aunty's help. The kitchen was a smallish square space; however everything was in a precise order. The sausages were being defrosted in the microwave, the eggs were out of the fridge (apparently best for sunny side ups!), tomatoes were halved with precision and sprinkled with a dash of salt and pepper ready for the oven. The toast of choice was the Sainsburys' brown loaf, which was ready to go in the toaster. I thought of helping with the mushrooms when Uncle commanded that the pan had to be hot and they had to be cooked in butter – not oil!

I followed his instructions meticulously since I knew the consequences were high stakes; having to rewash the same dish. A few other 'customers' (as Uncle lovingly called us) loitered in and out of the kitchen, each wanting to know when the food would be served. Each one of us knew that everything had to be perfect, 'as per Uncle'. It was futile to rush him.

After half an hour, when things were nearly done, Uncle did request his housekeeper, Mary, to prepare the teapots for English breakfast tea. Mary promptly boiled the water and poured it in the cups to rinse them, to keep the warmth, and then finally the tea was brewed to perfection.

The breakfast finally arrived, and I don't remember anyone appreciating his hard work, since it had been an hour that the flavours of the bacon, sausages and bread had been tantalising everyone's tongues. The joy and happiness in Uncle's face was vivid and he welcomed everyone to enjoy the breakfast.

As we devoured the hearty breaky, Uncle announced that dinner would be his famous Chicken Biryani and each of the members who had travelled from all over the UK for the weekend stay would have to savour it before they left. In addition, he planned to invite a few of his friends who were committed to his biryani experience. The excitement was enormous as all wanted it, and yet knew it was Sunday and most of us had to leave, some even had to drive for a few hours in the cold winter. Uncle didn't wait for the discussion and promptly asked me to join him for shopping. I was always the curious, enthusiastic girl amazed at his multi-faceted personality.

Before we proceed, I have to tell you a little bit about 'biryani'. The dish is described in the Cambridge dictionary as 'a dish from South Asia consisting of rice, meat, fish, vegetables and various spices'. However, the description really mars the essence of this regal dish, likely originating in Persia, but brought by the Mughals to India. The dish contains high quality rice as the main ingredient and you can add varieties of meat, fish or vegetables. The spices are exotic or simple and there are innumerable variations and styles to making biryani.

However, there are a few ingredients which are a 'must' to create the most authentic biryani; passion, love, patience and precision. Uncle had it all!

The recipe was from his Pakistani patient, an aged woman of eighty-nine years who treated him to her creation, and Uncle couldn't stop asking her for the recipe. In the initial years in the UK, he was a basic cook, but gradually his passion for food made him a passionate chef. His signature dish, 'Uncle's

Biryani' as we all address it even now, was ready to be created.

Uncle prepared biryani with laborious love. And accompanying him in his culinary journey was a treat to your senses. Uncle started by marinating the chicken pieces in yoghurt for thirty minutes. He washed the rice gently, in cold flowing water, and drained it in a strainer. The rice was cooked for twenty minutes and then drained and washed to stop it from further cooking. The big biryani pot was washed and ready to go on the stove. He put a generous quantity of oil (cooking for twenty people) and allowed the oil to warm up gently. Then he added in a huge amount of horizontally sliced onion and roughly smashed garlic. Into the mix went peppercorns, cinnamon sticks and bay leaves. The onions had to be translucent when he poured in the chicken and sealed it. Next, he added a few cans of diced tinned tomatoes and a medium tube of tomato puree, salt as required and chopped chillies. The aroma was delightfully spreading throughout the house and neighbourhood.

I stood next to Uncle taking precise instructions for layering whilst the meat cooked in a slow flame for over an hour, occasionally being stirred gently. Once the chicken was cooked about three-quarters, Uncle was pensive. He declared it was the most important stage, layering the biryani rice into the pot without mashing each long grain. He didn't trust any of his helpers to do it and finally combined all the ingredients together with meticulous love and care. Then he tightly sealed the pot and put it over a large tray partly filled with water. This was to ensure the biryani was cooked at a very slow heat to absorb the maximum flavour. He called out, finally, that all the food would be served in an hour. The wait was traumatic; we were ceaselessly salivating, and some started munching on appetisers. The clever ones waited patiently.

Finally, the time came and we all savoured, in big portions, the piping hot, delicately spiced Uncle's signature biryani. What remained for me is the memories of my special Uncle.

I am teary-eyed thinking of him. My heart brings in a quote from Rumi to describe him: 'Wherever you are, and whatever you do, be in love.'

Uncle loved unconditionally and lived from the heart. Even the food he created was a signature of divine laborious love.

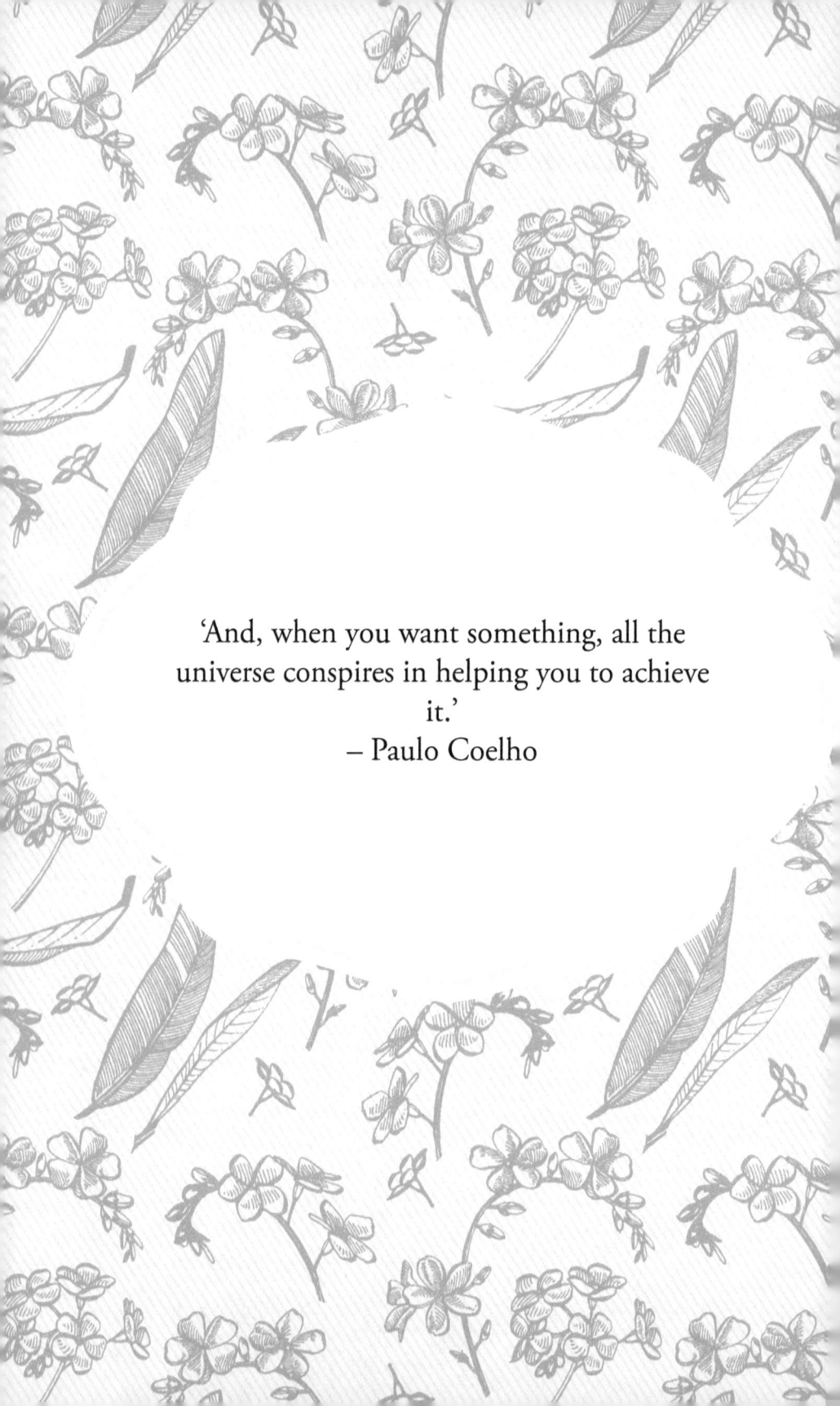

'And, when you want something, all the universe conspires in helping you to achieve it.'
– Paulo Coelho

THE KOOKABURRA CONNECTION

It's been a month and I'm still listening on repeat to Gabrielle Bernstein's *The Universe Has Your Back – Transform Fear to Faith*, on Audible. This is her second book I've read, and something about her personality or story telling reminds me of myself. I was so grateful and elated when she instantly replied on Instagram after I'd congratulated her on the success of her book, *Super Attractor*, a few months prior.

The chapter which draws my attention, on repeat, is 'The Universe speaks in mysterious ways'. The more I listen to the chapter, it compels me to write my experiences of communicating with the universe; sometimes a monologue and sometimes in dialogue.

As I sat on my meditation mat a few months ago, I asked for a sign from the universe that if it was listening to me and seeing my efforts, it should communicate. Sometimes it was roses, butterflies, rainbows, but time and again, a bird appeared which looked like a Kookaburra. I've been in Australia now for over twelve years and have, hardly ever, paid attention to Kookaburras. Occasionally, when the boys were young, they pointed out to a sombre Kookaburra sitting with a side-glance on a branch. They educated me on how their vocals can mimic human laughter, to which I would roar in laughter in order to initiate a response from the rather pensive creature, but with no response, to my dismay.

I decided that from now on I would look out for Kookaburras. Initially, every biggish bird I looked at in my neighbourhood appeared like a Kookaburra and I was disappointed. But I did have the insight that it wasn't a game I was playing with the universe. As I delved more deeply into universal communication and started penning down my experiences, I realised I had many, especially in the last five years since losing both my parents. The vision of my mother's laughter as she was leaving her body, my dad's voice who spoke to me while I was in a grocery shop (a day before he passed away), saying to me, 'You will always be safe', and his wristwatch which appeared miraculously in my new Audi car on the very same day. My faith in the Universal language was being affirmed as I surrendered in my spiritual journey. As Gabby said in her book, 'the more relaxed and aligned you are to your nature, the more you will see miracles'. Universal signs are just one of them.

Kookaburras were everywhere. Sometimes I saw them in a branch or a light pole. Sometimes a solitary soul reached out in my back garden to join in my music lessons, with the same pensive glance. Some of them were in paintings in coffee shops and on social media. I was elated to see them. Sometimes I would desperately look for them, but this never worked.

Forget-me-not, my creative child, was in my heart ready to come out into the world.

I had a series of coincidences and synchro-destinies with my book-writing journey. I was going to meet one of the most famous publishers in Rockingham, who generously read my novice book proposal and a few chapters, asking for a catch up.

The morning looked brighter after a few wet days. I meditated as normal and asked for a universal sign to guide me into this new world of being an author. I had no idea how books are created, apart from being a part of a distant journey of a few close friends who had become authors. I enjoyed their journey and fame and loved reading their creations.

The sign, of course, was Kookaburras, and this time there were two of them sitting in a tree. My ever-supporting husband and I got ready and drove down 50km south of Perth to Rockingham. The drive was nearly an hour long and the scenery transitioned from a city to a small-town feel. We arrived thirty minutes early and had decided to meet up in a coffee shop which had been suggested by Karen.

I felt a bit unamused, since there were no Kookaburras in sight, not even in the usual places I would find them in my neighbourhood. Yet I was not disappointed, and a deeper knowing arose within me asking me to surrender. I also earned the wisdom by reading spiritual books that not seeing the sign can also be a sign. And I needed to be more open-hearted about it.

We walked over fifty metres and found the coffee shop: a small, cute, vibrant shop, literally like a hole in the wall.

Adjacent to it, was a larger café called *The Laughing Kookaburra café*. I was now a little amused. I settled in a bench top opposite the café and my hubby went in to order our usual rounds of a 'small, extra hot, soy cappuccino' which was my latest fad!

I looked across the tables, a few of which were filled with people.

To my utter surprise, inside the café, were two large Kookaburra paintings in black and white, perched on gum tree branches. I felt a deep sense of knowing that my upcoming meeting was destined and guided by the universe. Within a moment I turned around and saw a bus, which stopped near me with a number plate of 555. I paused to look and recollected some angelic numbers which too were mentioned in Gabby's book! I thought to myself that this was just too much of a coincidence. Within ten minutes, another bus came by with a similar number plate showing the numbers 555.

I Googled the angel number, which said. '555 represents transition and welcoming change. Invite it with open arms.'

We eventually met Karen over coffee, and this is what happened!

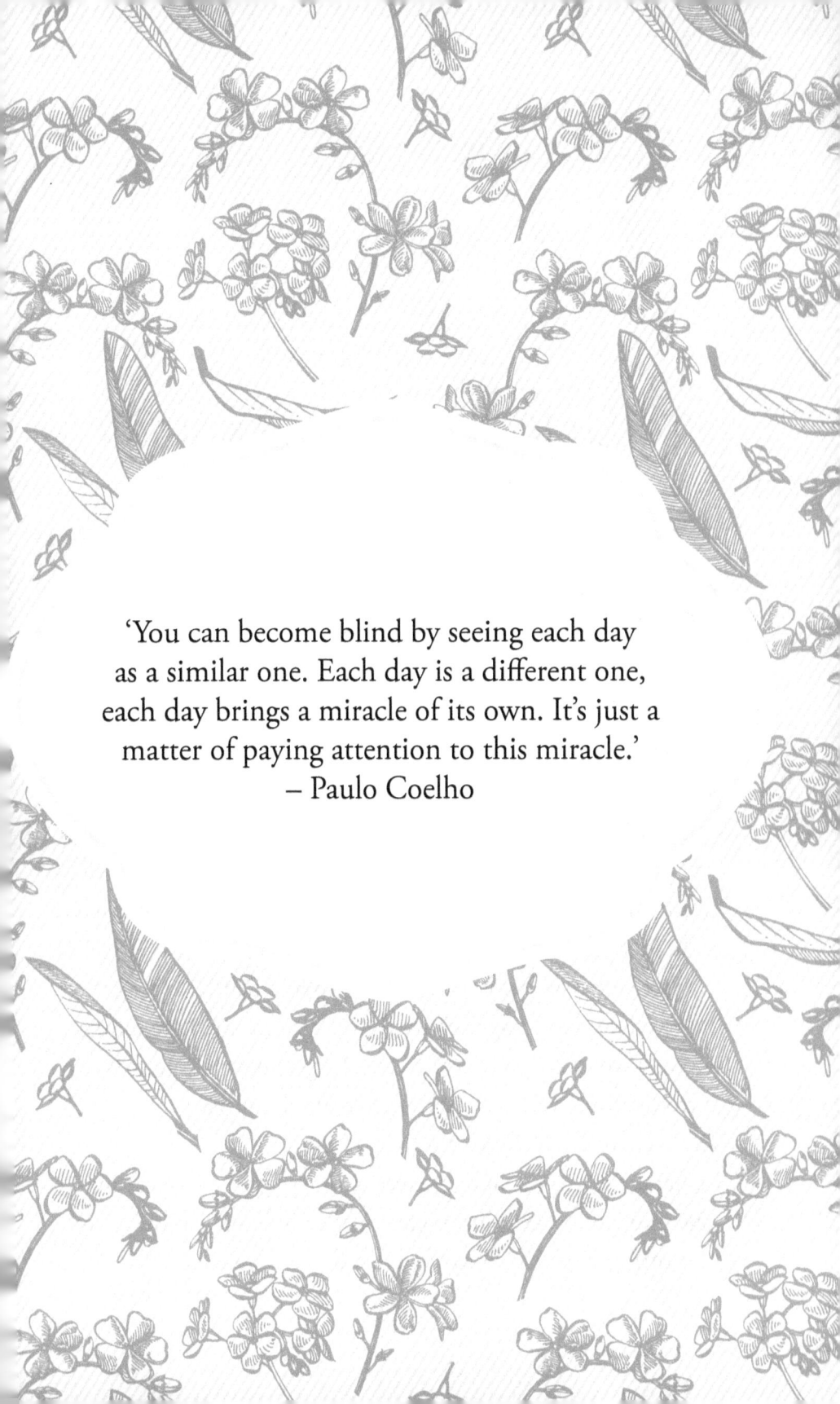

'You can become blind by seeing each day as a similar one. Each day is a different one, each day brings a miracle of its own. It's just a matter of paying attention to this miracle.'
– Paulo Coelho

THE LIGHT OF DARKNESS

The Victorian front door with solid oak panels and etched opaque glass with chrome fittings opened into a long, narrow corridor. An ornamental red-and-yellow-carpeted staircase on the right leads down to the first floor. Joyous voices welcomed us and lots of names were called aloud. Ananya stood timidly in the doorway, whilst a warm pair of hands hugged her close, touched her face and felt her features. Jay was nowhere to be seen and Ananya was nervous and annoyed, unsure of how to react. 'Is this my honeymoon?' she muttered to herself. 'This must be Aunty,' she thought.

The lady held her hands and took her in gently, feeling the side walls and judging each nook and turn to reach the dining room. Joyous laughter and hearty hugs followed and lots of introductions went on. Ananya was tired and jet-lagged and all this commotion added to her tiredness.

Jane, the delightful housekeeper, quietly picked up her luggage and announced; 'Room number 17 is yours. Up the stairs and turn to the left. Hope you like it,' she chuckled.

Ananya flung herself into the squishy bed which had thick duvets and soft pillows. She took a pause and looked at the ceiling which had some characteristic artwork which reminded her of being in Europe. Her eyes wandered left to look out through the double-glazed glass windows and was amazed to see the sunlight at 7pm. She looked right to see the small door which opened into a cabinet-sized washroom. She couldn't believe that things could be so petite and snug. For once she felt she was in the kingdom of Alice in Wonderland; yes – she was in England!

A Chippendale-style ten-seater mahogany dining table was the centrepiece of the dining room. The ends of the table and the pedestals elegantly carved in the characteristic Chippendale rope carving. The length and the width was not a fit for the smallish room but it spoke volumes about the owners. They loved open feasts where everyone could look at each other and share food and conversations which flowed across the table for hours. Ananya had no choice but to join in the party atmosphere, where all celebrated her as the new bride.

In the next few days, Ananya quickly navigated her ways into the seventeen-roomed Victorian town house and made friends easily with Jane, the housekeeper and Keith, the chauffeur. Uncle was busy at his surgery and had to go to work, since he had to fill his bag of stories for each evening. Jay was busy preparing for his exams, so Ananya spent a lot of time loitering around with Aunty.

Shadows of light and dark were all that Aunty's eyes could detect. Without colours in her new world, she had to work with textures, temperature, fragrance and her other senses.

Ananya closely observed how to peel and cut an onion, chop vegetables, wash and dry dishes, pack leftovers, change black bags, arrange a spice rack and make a cup of tea without being able to see.

She was taught how to open envelopes with a letter opener, how to touch-type on a Victorian typewriter, arrange books alphabetically in a library, and memorise cheque book numbers. She learned how to cook without seeing or tasting, just by the sense of smell, how to get the proportion of spice mix right for curries and biryanis, how to accurately cut meat and fish without battering an eyelid, how to recognise books by feeling them, how to touch a container and know what it contained, and how to recognise people by their footsteps.

Ananya's mind and heart opened to her newly married life, her new country, the new sensations, the new way of living and her new guide. The neurophysiological pathways in her brain exploded every night when she flung herself into her bed, overwhelmed with the knowledge she was challenged with.

She learned to tango and quick-step by counting, rather than the rhythm, and adapted to a new world which revealed secrets in every moment. She had to unlearn things which clogged her memory for the past twenty-four years and created space for the secrets which were continuously being revealed.

Aunty divulged her secrets each day and every story made her guess, observe, perceive, reflect and assume with a new perspective. At some point, she thought Aunty's life was delusional, with lots of speculation and hypothesis; the journey of an unprivileged, young determined woman, travelling to

Russia to pursue medicine, with bags full of stories of pain and betrayal, finally losing her eyesight, was surreal.

***

It had been eight years since she'd been there, after leaving for Australia some ten years ago. Ananya was attending a conference in the UK and she directed the driver to the address she knew by heart. She asked him to stop as she approached her destination. The 'sold' sign was partly covered in snow which she gently wiped off with her bare hands. She stared at the mansion with the eyes she had received as a wedding present some twenty years ago.

Now this pair of eyes finally saw the truth of 'Aunty'; an inspirational resilient teacher and story-teller. Most importantly she had cherished her twelve years of relearning.

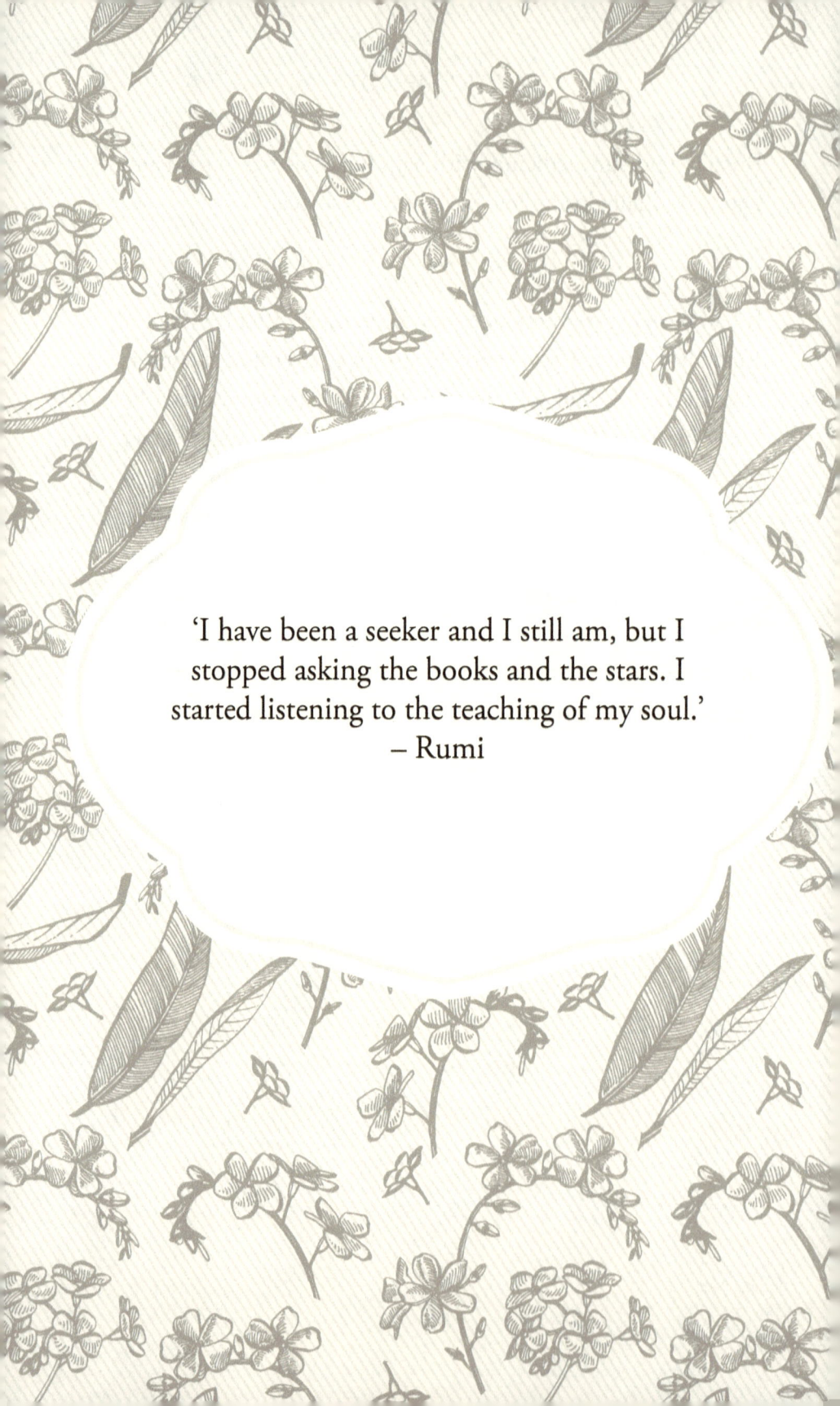

'I have been a seeker and I still am, but I stopped asking the books and the stars. I started listening to the teaching of my soul.'
– Rumi

THE MAGIC HUG

Bollywood connection!
I dropped the boys early to school as they had their annual sports carnival. I reached the hospital well in time, by 7.30am, and decided to settle in and have a cup of tea. Perth is still wintery in August, and although the days were getting brighter, there was a chill. The brightly coloured red bottlebrush flowers were blooming everywhere, and it indeed was a colourful scene.

I went to the upstairs tearoom close to my office and put the kettle on. I saw a cleaner, who we now refer to as 'patient support service workers' clearing the nearby bins. I remembered that lately I had noticed my office bins were not being emptied regularly, so I politely asked him if he was in charge of cleaning our offices too. He had a very pleasant demeanour and informed me it was not his area of service. But he did say that the other side of the hospital is cleaned on alternate days and that was the reason for the delay.

I thanked him, sipped my tea and went in to say hello to

my secretary before reaching my office. To my surprise the gentleman was there clearing my bin!

I was a bit embarrassed and informed him that it was not necessary for him to go out of his way. He pleasantly smiled and said it was his pleasure. As he was walking out of my office, he paused to read my name on the door and asked me if I was from India. Reading my surname aloud he also guessed the state from which I belonged. I was surprised and wanted to know more about him. I requested he take a seat, which he was reluctant to do initially, but I insisted. He informed me that he was an Anglo-Indian by birth and was born in Bangladesh. He studied accountancy and then went to Pakistan to study economics. He'd worked as an accountant for over fifteen years in Australia and then went on to do some business with cranes, which had had a $2 million turnover in just five years. The business suffered heavy losses with the wrong partners and so he moved on to travel the world for a while. He had then invested in a garment business with a friend in Malaysia and was cheated by one of the co-partners. He was offered a desk job again in accountancy which he didn't enjoy. Finally, one of his friends asked him to join the patient support services, predominantly cleaning hospitals. He said passionately, 'I love to help the nurses. They are often so busy with their scheduled tasks. I try and give a hand to draw the curtains or help the patients move around. This gives me a lot of peace, although I know it's not really my job.' He also claimed proudly that his wife was a registered nurse.

Alan was around seventy years old, with a pleasant face and a calming grin. He had a lovely personality and a warm energy. I was so grateful to have met him, accidentally, on that Thursday morning. It was a very warm conversation. I informed Alan that there was so much I learned from him in those fifteen minutes; the 'dignity' of labour, the commitment to enjoy whatever you do and to 'let go' of your failures and your past. He was thrilled and left my room thanking me with a bright smile.

This reminded me of what I had learned from an iconic Bollywood movie from the late 90s called, *Munna Bhai MBBS*. The movie had the typical recipe of a super-hit, blockbuster Indian movie, with musical numbers, glamorous costumes for the female actors, dramatic love stories featuring handsome male actors, lavish sets, elaborate dance sequences and comic relief provided by pratfalls or slapstick humour.

However, the movie was unique, since it explored social customs and traditional work culture around a prominent medical university hospital in Mumbai. I fondly remembered the scene where the lead male actor hugged a hospital cleaner and thanked him for doing a critical job central to patient care. This not only highlighted the dignity of labour but also sent a sublime message to respect everyone who contributes, in their own way, to running an organisation. The scene became iconic, and it was called 'The Magic Hug'. The concept of the hug went viral and became a cult amongst young and old, to convey compassion, support and love. Movies can have a huge impact, spreading positive messages and healing societies. I too felt the same emotion of happiness and gratitude after meeting Alan and thanking him for the work he does behind the scenes.

'We carry inside us the wonders we seek outside us.'
– Rumi

THE WHITE ROOM

I woke up to the chirping birds and a cup of light tea. It was one of my intermittent fasting days, something I was recently trying out. The feeling of waking up has always been a bit rushed in our household; doctors and their intense commitment to work! Currently to add to it, was a conscientious Year 12 student, my first born, Adi. Arry, being the second born and having a cucumber-cool attitude, often escaped all the chaos.

However, today, I woke up feeling special. I was excited yet calm and my usual nervous energy meandered me into gratefulness. I went straight to our 'White Room'; a special haven for my thoughts, emotions and energies. It's a lounge which gets the sun's full attention and has the charm of a conservatory. The tall French-glass doors are adorned with silk curtains with a pattern of red flowers on a bronze base. The furniture is artistically carved in pure white wood; French décor, with a Russian twist of matted-gold cushions! The white display cabinets hold priceless memories, some of which are antique and some trendy. And if you have a keen eye, you'll notice some miniature figurines I collected from car boot sales in the UK, some twenty-five years ago. In contrast to this, there is a unique signature collectable antique vase from China, meticulously hand-painted, in a delicately carved side table. A tall white unassuming lamp, with LED bulbs, warms the room when the sun denies its attention. The black wooden oak floor is covered with a generous off-white-grey-bluish tinge rug, lightening the room further.

My meditation mat is the center piece of the room. A rounded large cushion in a traditional Indian pattern of blue, white and red with various geographical shapes with a vision of a kaleidoscope. The dangly small pompoms are the highlights and how I love to sit in it!

On the east of the room, 'feng shui' guided, I have a white elegant wooden mantle with a few heads of the Buddha in golden hue. The center piece of the eastern wall is a hand-crafted medium-sized Ganesha; the Hindu Elephant God. This is carved in cement and polished in porcelain by a traditional village craftsman. I remember buying it some ten years ago in a local market fair, during one of our annual visits to India. The finish of the piece is so immaculate, it makes you wonder in awe at the power of creativity. Both symbolises wisdom. The ability of humans to reveal divinity into matter is as unique as quantum physics, when energy changes matter and you can create anything you want. This room is called 'The White Room' in the Baruah household.

A sleek smart TV, with the latest applications, adorns the northern wall, tastefully fitted into the décor of the room. The purpose of the room was not only as a meditative sanctuary, but for creativity too. A room where I could engage in writing, music lessons, yoga and dance routines.

As I ponder on the question of finding balance in our daily living, I look around me. The white room portraying duality echos balance. I looked further outside the French doors to see the young saplings, which were recently planted, surrounded by established trees. I realise how the delicate balance of nature is needed for healthy growth. I reflect on similar examples in all facets of life.

The Buddhist teachings seem to simplify this concept of developing a balanced approach to living. The Dalai Lama quotes: 'A gentle and skillful approach, taking care to avoid extremes, applies to healthy mental and emotional growth.'

The white room inspires me to deeply connect with myself. This in turn allows me to think flexibly, discover new perspectives and reflect on wisdom.

Life is a duality; the yin and the yang. The shiva and the shakti has to be in a coherent union for balance. Similarly, a modern and traditional room decor, antique and modern pieces, humble and extravagant collections, red and white colour, Buddha and Ganesha, meditative and high energy creativity, can all be in harmony with the Tao.

'If the light is in your heart, you will find your way home.'
– Rumi

TRUST ME, I WILL BE THERE

Rina knew the day would be hard to cope with. She had plans to ensure she remained busy, just to take her mind off her thoughts. She tried to surrender but the pain of losing her love made her feel hopeless. Yet she had to turn it around, since she still had faith; faith and trust in her guru who had transformed her life over four years ago.

Wiping her tears, she set off early morning to spend her day in her guru's ashram in Bangalore. The city was new to her, but her desperation to erase the day from her memory was so strong, she feared nothing. Her tears didn't stop, she submitted to her fate, but couldn't come to terms of why she had been betrayed.

Her broken heart needed some solace and she tried connecting with people. One of them was an acquaintance, Ronny, who happened to be a co-disciple of her guru. Lately, they were both enjoying a strong connection and Ronny showed undue fondness towards her. She didn't resist the flow of friendship and was completely unsure of how things would evolve. But she had a deeper knowing that she might be able to trust him.

The morning celebrations in the Ashram began with prayers to the God of Strength, Shiva. Rina couldn't stop her tears, but her strength was her guru. She completely surrendered her pain and let out her emotions, screaming at the glimpse of her guru. The Divine sight didn't give her peace, but there was assurance. Rina spent the entire day praying to the Divine and transmuted her pain to surrender.

The day was long; it was this day her lover was getting married to someone else. Everything in the world that day seemed to move in slow motion. She needed to get out of her restless mind. She called Ronny who happened to be in the same town and planned to meet up for the *International Satsang* in the evening. Satsang is a gathering of devotees who celebrate life through joyousness, seeking truth and divinity. Ronny promised to meet her at the satsang.

The satsang was to be held some 20km out of town, at a rather quaint place. Rina travelled on her own, unsure of the destination, but had trust that Ronny would be there with her in the evening.

She prayed to her guru for her safety, since it felt a bit uncomfortable travelling to an unknown destination on the outskirts of town. She finally arrived, after changing a few buses and a rickshaw ride, popular in India.

The satsang was full of people, both Indians and international disciples of the guru, attending the function. The atmosphere was rife with high-level energy and the chanting and music was magical. It brought out a trance-like feeling in Rina and she swayed spontaneously to the rhythm. But she didn't know anyone there and tried to look for Ronny in the crowd. She desperately called him a few times but couldn't get through to him. She messaged him frantically, still no response! She ran in the hall, purposeless, self-pitying and aimless. In the midst of all this emotional commotion, there was the beat of the drums, chanting and singing the praise of the Lord and the guru. Rina ran into the crowd and became one with them. She flowed in dance; it was as if it was the only way her body truly knew how to cry. Her dance was healing her; a language of emotion that is so much more ancient than words. The Divine communicated with her own soul and others. Most of them were international disciples and she met a Malaysian guy on the dance floor, as they both quietly communicated in their own way. Language was limited. He spoke Malay and Rina conversed in English and Hindi.

When the satsang ended, she felt light but dejected. She blamed her guru for giving her up on the day when she needed him most. How could she be betrayed twice on the same day? Ronny never turned up. Her faith was wavering and her heart was heavy.

It was quite late at night and Rina felt insecure. It was time to go home, and the crowd was dispersing. She found the Malaysian guy trying to find his way out too and went to say a final goodbye. He was very polite and offered to help her get back to Bangalore. Rina was unsure to take a favour from a stranger, especially on a day when she had been betrayed twice already. Before parting, the Malay guy shared his email on a piece of paper and handed it to Rina and said he would be in touch. Rina too shared her email, aimlessly since she was preoccupied on how to reach home safely.

Finally, after liaising with a few local people, Rina found the buses she needed and was on her way home. The crumbled paper was in her hand. She opened it up dispassionately and read the name: RONNY.

Paralysed at the coincidence, she initially felt numb, but her recharged energy after the satsang gave her clarity. She bowed down in reverence to her guru and acknowledged that he never left her alone on that day. He was there …

***

A decade later, Rina narrated the story to me. She never realised the significance of the universal energy which guided her back to love.

Her prayer for truth was the pathway to love herself once again.

'When we practice loving kindness and compassion, we are the first one to profit.'
– Rumi

TSUNAMI OF KINDNESS

The antique Steinway symphony grand piano stood tall and regal in the midst of the high-ceiling lounge. Children, aged between five and nine years old, scattered around the lounge giggling and laughing. One of them daintily sat on the piano stool trying to play a few chords. It was dusk and I went to pick up my seven-year-old Arry from Vera's piano class. I meandered my way through the lounge and peeked a little from the corridor but couldn't see Vera. Arry along with the other kids, were too distracted and having fun, and no one knew where Vera was.

Gently pulling my boy aside, I asked him to calm down as it was time to go home. He promptly informed me they were all having dinner and Vera was making a scrumptious chicken soup with bread. Before I could react, I saw beautiful Vera, always elegant and smiling, wearing a pure white apron over her well-fitted white shirt and denim jeans.

She greeted me with open arms and said that dinner was ready for the kids. The kids all jumped in to savour her soup and bread with dollops of butter. The scene warmed my heart, seeing hungry children eating with pleasure, joy and glee!

Vera offered me a coffee, but I politely declined since I could see that she had a busy job cleaning up after them. Before I left, I informed Vera that her gesture was kind, but it was not necessary to serve dinner to the kids after their piano lessons, to which she said that it was her pleasure, since she was cooking supper for her kids too and it was a very 'Ukrainian' thing to share food.

The lessons continued and the pick-up times were getting longer and more unpredictable, due to her commitment of feeding her students before they left. I didn't have the heart to discuss it with other parents but made some ground rules for my son to be picked up early.

I didn't know Vera well, apart from her piano teaching abilities. She had migrated to Australia from Ukraine and had completed a scholarship at UWA for advanced piano training. She was very pretty and radiated warmth and kindness. She was a dedicated piano teacher and loved her students earnestly.

It was December and the peak of summer in Australia. The piano lessons were becoming few and far between due to school holidays and social commitments. My seven-year-old was busy packing Christmas hampers for close family friends, but he insisted we get a real big hamper for Vera.

I asked him what goodies he would want to buy, to which he insisted we should gift her grocery vouchers, oil, bread, salt, sugar and some basic stuff. I was shocked at his suggestion knowing how kids love all the cookies, cakes and candy canes. My son explained that during the last six months that he'd been learning piano, he had noticed that Vera barely had anything in her pantry, yet she would make a simple meal with whatever she had and fill their bowls for supper. Some days, she would miss a meal if there wasn't enough.

I decided to meet Vera over a cup of coffee to learn about the person behind the mask of 'piano teacher'. She disclosed she was going through a very rough patch in her life. She had become penniless and had to work extra hard to maintain the kids and the house. She did multiple jobs throughout the day, and in the evenings, she was the dedicated piano teacher, teaching music through joy and love. I asked, 'Why do you make food for the kids? They do not expect it and neither do they need it.'

She gently replied, 'Since I had to make supper for my own kids, how could I not share with the others? They all love my food!'

And I asked her, 'But you went hungry?'

To which she shyly nodded, 'Sometimes …'

We took a hamper for Vera at Christmas filled with our love. I knew it was not enough to solve her problems. Her kindness was a tsunami that filled our lives and hearts, and we could only pledge to stand by her in her dark days, to see her emerge successfully.

Humans like Vera make this world a better place. These random acts of kindness fill our hearts with warmth and love. This, in turn, inspires us to be kind and generous. The feeling of making someone feel good is indescribable. It's a feeling to be cherished. Vera's act of kindness was without any expectations and this came back to her tenfold. She is happily settling now into her new life, managing a vibrant coffee shop, surely giving out free cake samples (!) and of course continuing her first love – piano.

'Set your life on fire. Seek those who fan your flames.'
– Rumi

WI-FI: THE DIVINE PORTAL

'I have been transferred to a rather small beach town in West Bengal.' The phone line was crackling and Tina could hardly hear what Debu had to say. She tried to keep the conversation going, in spite of the poor connection, thinking that Debu would be rather lonely and sad with this sudden job change. Tina reconnected the phone a few times and finally they both decided they would chat later.

Tina was always caring , especially towards her school friends. The bond was being reconnected after a good decade and a half. Tina and Debu were a dynamic duo in school. Both had a mischievous, fun-loving personality and were adventurous in their own little ways. They were both studious, yet often distracted the class with their jokes and mimicry. They escaped a fair bit of routine class work, some purposeful and some was their liberty. They were busy enhancing their school's position with their extra-curricular activities.

Their eyes shared their secrets and jokes were communicated just by looking at each other. They were also very different in their ways. Debu was a sport fanatic and an animal lover, and Tina was the creative fairy-tale princess. Their paths separated after school, and both went to pursue their chosen career.

Time flew inbetween and there were a few occasional letter exchanges between the duo. Tina was studying medicine in the UK and Debu established a career in Zoological sciences in India. A decade passed by and they lost touch.

In the early 2000s, social media was up and running. Firstly Orkut, then Facebook, both revolutionising friendship. People were super excited, particularly our generation. However, the duo didn't seem to catch up on social media.

Tina relocated to Australia after twelve years in the UK. She decided she needed a relaxing break at home before she started work in her new home. She took her young boys to India and planned to spend six weeks with her folks. As she started settling in, there was a desperate urge to connect with her old school and college mates. Tina was curious to know about them, especially her long-lost 'very good' friends. Debu was topmost in her mind, and after a few phone calls she found out she was, indeed, in the same city of Kolkata, in India, where Tina was staying. With excitement, she called Debu's number and spoke with utter enthusiasm. She was keen to meet up with her. Debu had mixed feelings (as confessed by her later on) but she too was curious to meet with Tina after twelve years!

They chatted the whole night and confided their life stories. Some were amusing, some sad and some complex. What was surprising was the short span of time in which they exchanged their life events. The next morning, they were like school buddies again, each knowing what the other needed to say or do.

The uniqueness in this friendship was that both had evolved mentally, emotionally and spiritually through different circumstances life had offered them, some of which were polar opposites. This not only connected them more, but they became mentors, teachers, spiritual guides and stalwarts for one another.

Debu was trying to settle into a small beach town after being promoted. Her current job was rather dull compared to the busy, multi-tasking portfolio she'd handled over the previous ten years in a big city. Everything was a challenge, but the duo believed that challenges were opportunities in disguise. The chats continued daily for hours, sometimes three to four times a day. From sorting out a safe home, to how to adapt into a village setting with bare amenities, to finding wonders in the sounds of the ocean, they helped each other to change their mindset to abundance. As they chatted frequently, their experience of life expanded. Debu narrated stories of the love and simplicity of the villagers and Tina embraced them with love. They analyzed serious situations over their phone chats and WhatsApp calls to find pertinent solutions. Some of these solutions worked and others were disastrous; they both decided it was a learning experience, 'so never mind.'

Four years passed, with Debu living in the small village town and she had made significant contributions, not only to her work, but also to the community. She raised awareness for environmental cleaning, uniting community groups, schools and local government. She was passionate about it and plunged in to create initiatives of beach cleaning in her own ways, with help from the local authorities. Her passion to never give up on a project, no matter how big or small, made her the person she is. She committed to take the 'sustainable clean project' with more vigour and passion into her newly promoted role, back in her headquarters, Kolkata.

***

Debu truly follows the principles of spiritual success; her dharma to serve, her intention to make a difference. Her detached attitude to surrender is her magical mindset.

Debu has positively influenced not only my life, but that of innumerable others. She guides and listens to others without judgment.

Our phone calls, chats and discussions are priceless motivation courses for self-transformation, laughter therapy, cognitive therapy and overall holistic friendship. Wi-fi, the 'divine portal', as I call it, has surely made this possible in this millennium.

'Don't grieve. Anything you lose comes round in another form.'
– Rumi

THE 10-YEAR-OLD MESSIAH

The flight to Bangkok was in the early hours of the morning. The kitchen was busy with Arry baking his famous chocolate brownies and cookies. Sunny made sure the passport and the tickets were all sorted, and he helped packed my bags. Adi wandered around Mum, not sure how he could add some comfort.

I tried to explain to Arry that Dimma (grandmum), might not be able to savour the goodies he'd made since she was in a lucid state. Although I, too, deeply hoped she could savour a bite since she enjoyed every aspect of life!

I was ready to let her go and liberate her from her pain. Ma had battled cancer for nearly eighteen months. This journey evolved each one of our family members in different ways. But it was the predictable phone call from my brother yesterday, who had said she might soon succumb to her ultimate human destiny.

The human emotions are weird. They always play with duality. They are really 'thoughts in motion'. They express themselves in many different ways. And yet one wants the best one to come up and not disturb you. We are constantly looking for peace and harmony in spite of the storm within. I was certain about Ma's certainty – but was uncertain about us. I was happy for her to be liberated, and yet there was a sadness that sucked me in. I prayed for wisdom to engulf all sadness and liberate us all.

Over the past eighteen months, I had continued to look for peace and guidance. I prayed relentlessly, meditated, attended spiritual retreats and read voraciously. Somehow nothing gave me peace. I looked for that 'particular message' which would open my heart out to liberate Ma.

I knew I was growing, and as we know, growth is always uncomfortable. The pain fractured our family and bonded us in various ways. The feeling of being rootless was undefinable, but we all prayed that Ma could reach her destination pain free.

Dinner was done and I was ready for an early morning flight the following day. It would be one of the strangest journeys of my life. I did have a rather blank emotion and was not trying to think too much. My ten-year-old son, Arry, insisted we go for a walk outside to get some fresh air. We both walked in front of our home, a slightly uphill wide road, which was dimly lit.

He initiated the conversation wondering how I planned to greet my Mum knowing it might be my last meeting. He kept talking and said, 'You look so sad. Would you like me to look like this when I visit you on your deathbed? Or would you want to see my smiling, peaceful face? You should know that the soul is eternal. Our bodies are just like garments.' He kept on repeating – 'Dimma isn't going anywhere, it's only her body. Just like we shed clothes, she too is doing the same, and now she is ready for a new one.' He also insisted that, 'We too have to shed our clothes and it's not sad at all. We can always feel her, only we can't see her. So, you better have a smile on your face and don't let her die before her death. She shouldn't see the sadness in your eyes. And know for sure that she will always be there with us.'

His words brought tears to my eyes, but I felt immense freedom. There was a deeper sense of knowing. The universe had sent 'him' as a messenger to guide me when I needed support most. All my desperation and apprehension faded, and I had this indescribable peace. I was now geared to meet Ma with all my energy and enthusiasm as I always did.

Whilst waiting in the airport lounge, I realised I was desperately looking for peace over the last 18 months. However, I didn't have the wisdom to see it. Now my vision had clarity to accept the reality. What I also realised, after saying goodbye to Ma is, 'Suffering disappears, and all that remains is love.'

'Whatever lifts the corners of your mouth, trust that.'
– Rumi

THE BOND BEYOND

Scene 1:
It was a concrete flight of stairs with roughened edges. That didn't stop us from jumping alternate steps and creating our own synchronised movements with our hands. We were coordinated and graceful, though at times a bit wobbly. The songs were made spontaneously, and we were in wonderland. The games were only known to us and we giggled when our parents stopped by. We lived in a world of imagination full of boundless freedom. We were three years old and grew up together in the neighbourhood. Our paths evolved in separate ways, but the bond strengthened throughout our journeys of life.

After five decades, we still share every pain and pleasure. We still take each other for granted, knowing well, all will be forgiven. We have 'sorry' and 'thank you' at the tip of our tongues knowing that this bounty is too precious. In spite of the distance, the challenges and triumphs bond us together, along with the primary game we shared and created when we were three. This game is magical and unique which enabled us to stay in each other's hearts, sharing this timeless bond called 'best friendship'.

Scene 2:

The laughter was totally inappropriate! We couldn't decipher what made us giggle at the news of a friend's granny's death. Was our emotional intelligence so low as twelve-year-olds? Why couldn't we express our empathy at the appropriate time? We were team captains and led the girls through various house competitions. We bonded them together, were inclusive and had fun in school. We were girls of the 80s; innocent and gullible with no self-obsession. Then how could we be so insensitive? We apologised promptly for the giggles and till today couldn't fathom out the reason for our immaturity. We often blamed it on hormones.

Now as quadragenerians, we haven't changed much. Laughter is our accessory. We realised that laughter is full of warmth and life. It is genuine and sincere and heals our souls.

We finally found a reason for this beautiful thing called laughter – old friendship.

Scene 3:

'Are you waking me up to say your ex called you on your birthday?' She promptly said, 'yes' and was unapologetic. She reminded me of how her mum had secretly followed her and her boyfriend and the massive stories I had to generate to cover for them. I couldn't stop reminiscing about our medical school days. We both went straight to the fun times we had in the dissection hall and the college canteen, as well as how we chatted all night and missed classes the next morning.

We spoke about our crushes and the disappointing break-ups. We laughed remembering some of our quirky teachers and our disastrous dealings with patients when we first started.

Our stories seemed to rotate around the liveliness of the college days; the free hours, Sundays, the chatter and the freedom of being away from home.

We had unpalatable stories of being a 'fresher' in university; long hours of study, totally drained brains and inedible food. We didn't discuss how unprepared we were to live independently at eighteen, messing up our finances and unhealthy eating, along with our immature and careless decisions.

But what we remember fondly is the pure, carefree fun we had, with no responsibilities. We were free in our hearts and our souls. In spite of our current busy lives, we take time out occasionally to refresh ourselves with stories like these, which nourish us with pure happiness in friendship.

Scene 4:

Driving at 80mph and 'swaying' is in no way good on a freeway. We tried to stop but we couldn't. Even dangerous driving and real death were not inhibiting us. It was a crazy moment! We were trying hard to stop our unrestrained laughter, but our outbursts continued.

We decided to stop the car and take a break. The topic we laughed at was unplausible and when we finally stopped our aching bellies, we wondered why we were laughing so hard.

Our friendship had developed over the previous twelve years, in a new country, as migrants.

***

We have some things in common, but our personalities are strangely different. However, we merge cohesively to form a bond. We have proof of the depth of our friendship, since we support each other in the challenges of our lives. We spend whole days together doing school pick ups and drop offs, walks, yoga, grocery, laundry, lunches – chatting, venting, laughing. For hours in our days, we are maskless, being just ourselves. We don't need mirrors on those days.

We have passed trials and could go into battle for each other. We really don't know what makes us laugh. Sometimes we can just look at each other and catch the tail of a joke. Sometimes, we role-play or mime, creating imaginative scenarios to create a hearty laugh. We have earned this bond with steady steps that built trust. Friendship is a precious kind of love and I pray that all friendships span this lifetime.

'What you seek is seeking you.'
– Rumi

A PERMISSION SLIP ...

'Yes my dear, it's okay for you to put your feet in this warm footbath. The smell of lavender will calm you down and the warmth of the water will rejuvenate your nerves and improve your circulation. I can feel that your breath is slowing and you are gently settling your body into a comfortable position. You can sway and the subtle movements in your body are indeed helping you to be mindful. You are now feeling grounded on the seat whilst your heart lifts up. The feeling is gentle, yet profound.'

I can now allow myself, with compassion, to hear the shower that's been running for over ten minutes in my teenage boy's bathroom. I can hear the thunder and the muffled music coming from the lounge, but nothing is bothering me. I can feel the breath in my belly and the sensation creeping up my calves. My gaze is a stare, as my mind has a sublime curiosity of what's happening within and around me.

I allow my thoughts to come and go and don't blame myself for the chatter. I allow even my fearful, nervous thoughts about my son's exam, yet don't want to cling to them. They pass without hesitation and remorse. I had thought they might linger, and I waited for a moment, conditioned by habit, but they gave me permission to let go. I thought to myself that thoughts, too, can be so kind, so why do I fight them?

I pay attention to my breath; the thread which keeps me alive. I pause and feel the sensation of my breath going in and out, wondering to myself, 'who is breathing?' There is no answer, but a felt sensation. I try to catch it wherever it moves; sometimes in the tip of my nose, sometimes my belly and sometimes my chest. After a while, it consumes my whole body.

The footbath has cooled so I pat my feet gently dry and apply a luxurious foot cream with 25% shea butter, bought just a few months ago to caress my feet. It is now finally doing a good job of nourishing my peds. I love my cute pair of pink socks, completing my night-time routine by wearing them.

Slipping into my bed, I continue writing the permission slip. I love myself with all my flaws and talents. I acknowledge that I am unique and exclusive. There is no one else like me. I understand myself, my emotions, my pains, my experiences, my flaws and my victories like no one else can. I share them with you all, but why do I expect you to absorb them like I do?

I give myself permission to appreciate all the beauty I have within me, which radiates throughout the world. I forgive myself for my misconceptions and mistakes. I applaud my commitment to learn and improve myself, every day. I give permission for myself to feel happy, scared, anxious, excited, sad, joyful, free or trapped. 'It's all okay, my dear. Choose yourself because it isn't selfish, it's the most important thing you could ever do to honour your heart and soul.'

Have you noticed the delicate spring leaves in the branches of the trees? How gently they are looked after, by the mother-tree. They withstand all weather conditions yet show their strength in their vulnerability.

I give you permission to be vulnerable, to care for your gentle self, to forgive and forget, to let go.

I give you permission to choose yourself first and celebrate yourself, since this life is yours and you are here to live it. Applaud every step that allows you to climb to your highest peaks.

You are the Creator's enigma and the puzzle is encoded by the universal self – you!

'Your heart knows the way. Run in that direction.'
– Rumi

SLEEPING WITH A STRANGER

Some were white and fluffy, and some had a greyish hue, with a tinge of silver. They formed a perfect chorus of an orchestra in the azure blue sky. They floated so light, yet you could see some were heavy, ready to pour down. They were singing freedom but were uncertain when they would be free of their shapes and loosen themselves of the rain which would wet the earth. Anushka looked through the double-glazed oval window, which had a few icicles, before she pulled the shutter partly down.

She looked out and wondered what her reaction should be. Should she jump out of the plane at 35,000 feet or just get on with a life of uncertainty after hearing Raj's confession, that he hadn't had a job for over six months. He calmly comforted her by saying that she would be living with his uncle and aunt in Birmingham, until he sorted things out.

Anushka met Raj during their medical internship in Delhi, and their relationship had developed over a few months. Then

Raj flew off to the UK to enhance his medical career, with the promise that he would marry her when he got his first job. There was a year of painful separation, but they were in touch via the occasional international phone call and regular airmails. Well, that was the norm in the 90s! An unknown trust and faith bound the relationship, then and now …

It was daytime and Anuskha felt alien, since she had waved goodbye to her parents a few hours ago, in the midst of the dark night. Tired yet excited she was keen to absorb every experience and this was her very first time flying across continents. Raj was asleep though his hands held her 'mehendi' decorated hands tightly. She pulled away her bangles gently, so as not to hurt his hands, and quietly settled in her seat, unfastening her seat belt. It was a fortnight since their wedding and she was flying to an unknown destiny.

Anushka walked in the aisle for a bit and carefully looked at the vastness of the Boeing 747. She was gently guided by the KLM air hostess to her seat. She initially sat on the edge of the seat and gently started relaxing as a sign of surrender. Raj slept comfortably and she couldn't take her eyes off him. A deeper knowing, her inner guidance couldn't be wrong. She thought to herself, 'Does trust come before love or can both come at the same time?'

The strong affections and the energy you feel when 'in love' is a Divine connection. She remembered her favourite author Paulo Coehlo's words: *Love can consign us to hell or to paradise, but it always takes you somewhere.*' She gently took Raj's hands and fell off to sleep.

Birmingham was a busy city and everything was new for

Anushka. She was welcomed with open arms to Uncle and Auntie's home and became fervently busy meeting people and learning new skills. The new Raj, on the other hand, was constantly protecting, rescuing and nurturing her. Anushka had a vibrant enthusiasm for life, however she was always hesitant to step out of her comfort zone. She was keen to explore and experience new things but within her familiar zone, coasting through life. Raj, on the other hand, always took the road less travelled. He regularly stepped out of his comfort zone and ventured into unfamiliar territory, gathering new experiences and taking risks. He grew into a person capable of thriving, no matter where the journey might lead. Raj taught Anushka to take little steps and cross into the unknown, knowing that everything would be okay. They had their challenges and triumphs, familiarising into the new territory, but they learned how to successfully navigate it.

They thrived and lived in the UK for over a decade and were blessed with two boys.

Raj had an innate nature of being a stranger in a strange land and making that his comfort zone. This became wider when they migrated to Australia twelve years ago. Life is constantly changing and evolving.

It was a busy day in the Baruah household. They were all getting ready, especially Anushka, who couldn't decide on her hair style. The evening was dry and a pleasant 18 degrees, although the Perth winters can be wet. Champagne and rosé was being served to the guests at the entrance in delicate crystal flutes. The hall was beautifully decorated in hues of blue and silver. Warm hearty laughter and constant chatter were like music to the ears. The aroma of the food tickled the palate and the music reminded everyone of the golden 90s. Friends and family joined in from all over the world. Within a large circle of friends, Raj finally caught a glimpse of Anushka. She looked elegant and youthful, even after twenty-five years. He was very proud of his salt and pepper hair, since he claimed that for a mature surgeon, greys are the signature of his skill.

Anushka went around the room to meet her guests with open hugs. She opened her heart to them, as each one had made a contribution in their life journey. Anushka was familiar with Raj's classy style and appreciated how immaculately he carried his finest suits; today was no different. Their boys were very much a part of their parent's exciting story. They often felt that the risk in this love story was nerve-racking and gullible, but they had learned by living with them that, 'for those who love with love and soul, there is no such thing as separation' ~ Rumi.

The lights dimmed, the podium fell silent, the spotlight was on the couple. The rhythm of their heartbeats merged with the music and clapping of hands, as Raj led Anushka to the dance floor. They danced as if there were no tomorrow!

So, although trust is foundational in all human relationships, it doesn't always have to come first; it can come in a package deal called LOVE.

'Be grateful for whoever comes, because each has been sent as a guide from beyond.'
– Rumi

BOON COMPANION

She sold herself as unworthy, unimportant, insignificant and irrelevant. Married at seventeen to a man fifteen years older was a normal situation in the village. She was in a marriage where domestic abuse was common and she knew nothing else. She was illiterate, dependant and accepted this as her conditioned fate. But deep within, was a ray of hope to nurture her depleted self and to set herself free. Its called courage!

She expressed her desire to earn some money for herself to a man whom she trusted and fondly called her brother. He worked in the nearby town in a government office as a chauffeur and was aware of her misfortune. He had good intentions to support and help her, but opportunity was what they were waiting for.

Ms. Sapna Sinha was posted as a Chief Scientific Officer to upgrade the Aquamarine Museum in the small town of Digha. A lady of high calibre and experience, she was up for the challenge. The town had limited facilities and coming from an urban society she knew that this journey would need all her efforts, both professionally and personally.

The office quarter was a spacious three-bedroom apartment but had basic facilities. Her team upgraded her accommodation to the best level of comfort and security available within their means. The official staff were in total admiration and dedication, while a few were even fearful since she was a person with power.

Sapna's first requirement was a domestic caretaker. She called her staff to find a suitable candidate. Being a spinster, having a pet dog, Rani, and managing a highly demanding job, her priority was always to have efficient domestic help.

Within a few days of starting work, her chauffer brought in Laxmi for an interview as a domestic helper; a lady in her mid-twenties, simple and uncouth. Sapna conversed with her briefly and knew she was a novice, but somehow, her gut instinct told her that Laxmi needed her. Sapna promptly appointed her, not knowing anything about Laxmi except that she was a mother of two young boys and wanted to start earning some money for herself.

A few months of torture followed. The Indian summer was intolerable, with a non-functional air-conditioning unit in the apartment. Rani was falling sick frequently and Laxmi was overwhelmed learning Sapna's way of cooking and living. Sapna tried to escape to the city every weekend and questioned herself regarding her self-inflicted challenge and its worth. Given her stature, she could have easily taken a transfer to a position in a big city, but sometimes, one had to push boundaries to evaluate resilience, and that's exactly what she did.

She realised that what truly messed her up, was her expectations, especially when they were not met. She realised that radical self-acceptance was the path to take one's power back.

The next few months was a steep learning curve for both Laxmi and Sapna. Laxmi shared her life stories of abuse, neglect and insecurities. She was grateful to Sapna as a protector and guide. When one drops the pretence of perfection and simply show up as one's true self, one expresses courage to declare that each one of us are ordinary, struggling humans. Laxmi's authenticity allowed Sapna to open up with her stories of rejection, regret and failure. They both realised there was nothing to be hidden or ashamed of. This ripple effect of courage was powerful and liberating.

Laxmi was a keen and enthusiastic learner. She learnt how to read and write, operate household machinery, prepare low-fat healthy meals and keep the house spick and span, just as Sapna liked it. In addition, she learned about unconditional love, from the dog Rani.

Rani had been rescued by Sapna from the street just a year before, and she was the most important member in the household. In spite of Sapna being a vegetarian, Rani always got the best cuts of meat whenever Laxmi went shopping. She started praying and meditating with Sapna and tried to emulate her lifestyle and skills in her own way.

Her unconditional love also touched Sapna, who looked after all her minor needs, including a foot massage (completely undemanded).

Laxmi gradually showed some confidence in herself. She could now stand up to the domestic abuse in her own way and sometimes would not give up her rights. She still couldn't uproot herself from her family home, though, which she believed was her identity. Yet there were little steps of empowerment. Sapna on the other hand developed patience, dropped her over-reactivity and discovered a lot of her 'truths'.

A couple of years passed and both of them grew in their own ways. They were both depleted in areas of their lives which needed nourishing. They both invested in themselves, to be the best version of themselves.

Sapna and Laxmi are now moving on to their next destination. Being recently promoted as a director of her organisation, Sapna is migrating to the capital city, Delhi. In her valedictory speech, she not only thanked her staff for the successful running of the museum but thanked the universe for the opportunity to replenish herself.

This story reminds us that when we create relationships with an open mind, we get teachers, awakeners, connection seekers and allies, all in one. We imbibe gratitude for the life lessons others have taught us.

'Your kindness cannot be said.
You open doors in the sky.
You ease the heart and make
God's qualities visible.'
– Rumi

TEACHERS IN DISGUISE

The school bell rang and hundreds of children ran chaotically, surprisingly forming pristine straight lines for their assembly. The shrieks of laughter and the bond among the children brought the playground colours to a heart-warming hue. We caught a glimpse of the teachers and the elegantly dressed headmistress, about to address the assembly. Tina and I waited patiently outside the headmistress' office, since we had an appointment to see her soon after.

The school had a distinct reputation for academic excellence. Mrs Fernandez started the school some twenty-five years ago, in her home premises as a day school. A highly qualified person with academic accolades, who widely travelled the world, she had a vision to guide and empower young minds.

We were asked to sit inside her room, just after 9am and Tina looked calmer than me. We were both greeted by a firm, dynamic voice and Mrs Fernandez radiated a glow which engulfed us with warmth. She made Tina comfortable immediately, offering her a job as a teaching assistant for the pre-primary class. She clearly mentioned Tina's role as an observer, initially for the first few months, and then depending on her progress, would initiate her to her responsibilities. I was a bit taken aback knowing that my sister was supposed to have an interview with her that morning, before the job offer. We were new migrants to the town and had visited her once, at her home, to discuss potential job opportunities in the school. Tina had minimal work experience as a school assistant after leaving high school, but no formal teaching qualifications. However, like Mrs. Fernandez's vision, Tina too aspired to be a teacher at the prestigious school. Unaware of her limitations, Tina had the trust and belief that Mrs. Fernandez would take her under her guidance.

We were taken to look around the school by one of the teaching assistants.

We were elated but my mind wondered, 'On what basis did the headmistress make a decision to employ Tina, in this competitive world, to be a part of her team?' I had a big WHY on my mind. We started the tour with the pre-primary class and Tina was excited to see the smiling faces of the noisy three- to four-year-olds. Then we wandered around each classroom in the junior school. We were shown the staff room, the restrooms for the kids and the teachers, the school canteen, the music centre and the gymnasium. The playground appeared to be the heart of the school. Tina's eyes glittered with excitement and there was an unsaid pride which she displayed while visiting each area. She embraced the feeling that she was already a part of the school.

What amazed me, was not Tina's reaction, but what I

observed. I saw that in each classroom or facilities shown to us, there were helpers who had some form of disability, as the world labeled them.

Some had a limp or a stammer which we could see, and some had pain reflected in their faces, which they were trying to hide. I was astounded to see a school which thrived as one of the primary institutions in the state for academic excellence, but here was also an institution of humanity which enriched and nourished lives. The experience brought many emotions, but the one which was vividly evident on both of us, was gratitude.

Tina continued in the school initially as an observer, then as a teaching assistant and finally as a primary school teacher for twenty years. She was nurtured and nourished patiently, within her limitations. The school became her identity and she bloomed with confidence, pride and dignity. I continued to take an active interest, not just in the school, but the foundational rock behind it – Mrs Fernandez. I was intrigued with her compassion and magnetism and wanted to know her journey.

I visited her yearly, on my annual visits to India, and with each visit I continued to realise the power of kindness, compassion and humanity. The power of selfless service. The power of dedication and commitment, to help people who were not as fortunate. I directly questioned her regarding why she employed people who had limitations, not fearing the excellent reputation of the school. She fondly replied, 'Success depends on deepening our connection with others.' After multiple short conversations and interactions, I realised I was blessed to know a person who embodied empathy, not as a word, but as a technique. Mrs. Fernandez had the ability to appreciate others suffering and place herself in their shoes. She always tried to understand the background of people and then connected with them rather than being judgemental.

Several days later, on the same visit, I decided to drop into the nearby mall for shopping. I hired an autorickshaw and promptly realised he was taking a longer route and would overcharge me. The heat, pollution and the noisy crowd already made me impatient. Suddenly, I had an outburst and asked the driver to stop. I exploded and gave him a mouthful of my frustration, and how I realised he was taking a longer route to rip me off! The autorickshaw driver stared at me with a defiant expression and said that he was trying to get me there via the quickest route, since he was aware of roadblocks near the mall!

I paid him without a further comment and started walking. I couldn't drop my anger and frustration. After a twenty-minute walk, I reached the mall to find out that all the nearby roads indeed had road works. I stopped for a cold drink and fell silent. I did judge the autorickshaw driver and didn't practice Mrs. Fernandez`s principle of 'seeing things from another perspective.'

Tina had to take early retirement from school due to unforeseen circumstances at home. We lost both our parents over two years, but Tina's loss was significant since she lost her home and identity too. Mrs. Fernandez however went out of her way to make sure that Tina got a pension, and provided her with a reference, highlighting Tina's effort at improving her skillset. Although we moved on and Tina resettled in a new city, Mrs. Fernandez's genuine compassion continued. She frequently spoke to Tina, making time out of her busy schedule and guided her in her own way. She herself battled multiple health issues, which failed to deaden her spirit.

On my last visit, I met Mrs. Fernandez and passed on Mum's message, which Mum had failed to say aloud to her, clouded by emotions. Mum had said, 'I was not destined to see God in person, but I have had the opportunity to see God's ways in Mrs. Fernandez.' She chuckled gracefully listening to it and quickly brushed her tear-filled eyes and fussed over us while having coffee.

As many great spiritual beings have said, 'Your greatest teachers in life are the people whom you interact with.' I too had the opportunity to meet teachers in disguise, who enriched my soul.

As I write my reflections on the feelings of genuine, universal compassion, I realise that to enhance our capacity for compassion, we have to share the sufferings of others.

There is scientific research as evidence that developing compassion and altruism has a positive impact on our mental and physical health. This in turn opens our heart to warmth, friendship, affection and calmness. These conditions are absolutely necessary for happiness.

And Mrs. Fernandez is a living example of compassion – the real value of human life.

I can't forget my other teacher, my sister, Tina, who never gave up her dream of being a teacher, no matter how the universe reacted. We all have limitations in every aspect of our lives, but if we can aspire and visualise where we want to be, there is a genuine possibility to achieve it.

FORGET ME NOT

If one can surrender with faith and trust to one's guide or mentor as Tina did, everyone's own Mrs. Fernandez will be there, in their life, to hold their hand and emulate the Divine.

'If I love myself, I love you. If I love you, I love myself.'
– Rumi

ZEST FOR LIFE

We walked silently, amazed at the breathtaking floral displays. Hundreds of visitors attended the show each year. This was the 'Cut Section' exhibit and our eyes settled on the First Prize winner. Indeed, it was the pale pink floribunda blooms with a moderate sweet fragrance.

There were three in a tall crystal vase: a large, opened bloom at the top, a partially opened bloom in the middle and a large, pointed bud at the bottom. The leaves were large, leathery green and they had thick stems with large prickles. It was Ma's pride and privilege and she nurtured it with enormous love. It was the magnificent 'Queen Elizabeth' rose.

The Shillong Flower Festival was an annual spring event in our small town, a hill station in the north-east part of India. It was a five-day event organised by the local horticultural society and was a garden exhibition. Ma would eagerly wait for the show and put all efforts to get the best blooms for her exhibits. Ma was extremely proud of her small garden. A few months before the show, a helper would bring various types of organic manure to enrich the soil. Pots were painted and we had strict instructions not to touch anything.

Ma's garden was her sanctuary. She was an ardent gardener, with a green thumb; she could grow anything. I felt this was because of the balance she created as a gentle gardener. The role of nature is to assert herself and Ma cradled the life that dwelled within with pure love. She won innumerable prizes for her blooms but yet her favourite was the 'Queen Elizabeth'. I remember as a child how she roamed around our garden with her cup of tea, first thing in the morning. She always took time to stand beside the elegant 'Queen' for a while, admiring her in all her glory.

The Shillong home was sold and after thirty years, my parents moved to the eastern part of India, West Bengal. Ma's garden was uprooted and so was a part of her soul. She never settled in the new land and was always saddened about how 'Queen Elizabeth' didn't survive the move. She partly blamed herself for it, I thought, since she mentioned it in every phone call we had.

She established a garden in our new home with flora suited to the tropical climate, but her desire to grow something unique and challenging remained. On her last visit to the foothills of the Himalayas, she encountered a magical bloom on her climb down from a temple. The small, pink, wild blooms, a perennial herb commonly known as the 'Blue Rock Anemone,' stole her heart. Her passion to acquire a small branch to grow it in her garden made her interrupt a meditating sage, whose wrath she was ready to accept! She tried to nourish the plant in the tropical environment back home and was successful in her efforts.

She fondly told me that she would often speak to the plants to nurture them, to which I would smile. Later in life, I discovered there is scientific evidence that plants do communicate via vibrational frequency of energy. I now understand the mystery of why her soulful garden, was so vivacious and colourful. Her wait until midnight to photograph the bloom of the 'Queen of the Night,' a rare species of cactus which only blooms at night and wilts at dawn, asserted her passion, once again, to capture nature's magnificence.

Ma was adorned with a laugh which many people found extraordinary; a laugh which was effortless, humorous and climbed several octaves. It was infectious, and neighbours and friends recognised her laughter as her identity. She had a zest for life which was unaffected by challenges, of which she faced a fair amount during her life. She reclaimed her right to happiness by embracing music. She was a born singer and music was her external heartbeat. She often commented on the vibrations of music, which felt so heavenly, as if it was ethereal energy seeping into her. She listened to music from the start of the day, often annoying family members as it was just noise to for most. However, it was medicine for her, delivered in the most Divine way.

As her physical self gradually faded away into nothingness battling cancer, her hope to get better, explore the world and enjoy flowers and music, remained untouched. During her borrowed time, on her way to the hospital, she never missed a chance to see something which touched her soul; be it the fresh fruits decorated on the roadside stall or a flowering bush. These were her therapy to slightly ease her physical pain.

***

It's 23 September 2022 today and I am celebrating the birthday of the loving soul who was my Ma. I am reflecting on suffering and how it allows us to accept life's inevitable bitter truths. Although pain and suffering are a universal human phenomenon, we don't have an easy time accepting them. And I often wonder, 'how do we deal with life after losing a loved one?' There is no right answer for this, I guess.

For me personally, Buddhist teachings, especially those of the Dalai Lama, helped me to face and transform suffering. The story which I have to highlight is Kisa Gotami's search.

The story goes, that in the time of Buddha, a woman named Kisa Gotami lost her only child. Unable to accept it, she went to Buddha and asked for help to revive her child. Buddha replied calmly, 'Bring me a handful of mustard seeds from a household where no child, parent or servant has died.' She immediately rushed out to the village and began going from house to house in search of the mustard seeds. Kisa Gotami was not able to find a home free from the suffering of death. Seeing that she was not alone in her grief, she returned to the Buddha who said with great compassion, 'You thought that you alone had lost a son, but the law of death is that among all living creatures, there is no permanence.' Once we realise we are not alone, we no longer feel isolated, and it gives us some kind of condolence. This insight didn't take away my pain of losing my mother but helped me reduce my suffering and struggling against this sad fact of life.

Ma was not only a lover of nature, music and life but

enriched the lives of others in her own way. She unified with the Divine four years ago, but still every flower or garden speaks to me, reminding me of her love, which lingers as a smile.

The Eastern Hindu traditions believe strongly on rebirth and our journey as a soul.

I end this homage to my Ma with the words which are embedded in my soul:

> *'The soul migrates from body to body. Weapons cannot cleave it, nor fire consume it, nor water drench it, nor wind dry it.'*
> *– Bhagavad Gita*

ABOUT THE AUTHOR

Dr. Aparna Baruah is a consultant radiologist, currently working at Sir Charles Gairdner Hospital, Perth, Western Australia. She completed her bachelor of medicine and surgery from India in 1996, and migrated to the UK in 1998 to pursue further training. She now lives in Perth, Australia, since 2009.

Aparna has multifaceted interests and is currently pursuing music professionally. She has her own YouTube channel, which features her music videos. She is passionate about dance, yoga and meditation. As a multidimensional woman, mother of two, she has diverse interests with a parallel career in professional music. Aparna is passionate about engaging and inspiring the newer generation. She is a role model to show that one can pursue their passions and have a healthy work-life balance. Her mantra is: *Create the life you want in your vision board first*, and, *We can have it all.*

Her creative facets, along with her spiritual self, took her to an inward journey during COVID-19. The feeling of losing control as a doctor, as a human being and losing her parents, conceived this book. She wrote a collection of short stories, a catharsis for her soul, and was guided by intuition, synchronicities and a deeper faith.

Dr. Aparna Baruah is the author of the book *Forget Me Not,* a collection of short stories, and she is also a contributing author to *Women Leading the Way* published by Women Changing the World Press. Like the flower, the stories in this book embody good memories, love and joy.